Center for
Creative Leadership

Becoming a Strategic Leader

Richard L. Hughes
Katherine Colarelli Beatty

Becoming a Strategic Leader

Your Role in Your Organization's
Enduring Success

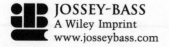
JOSSEY-BASS
A Wiley Imprint
www.josseybass.com

Center for
Creative
Leadership
NORTH AMERICA EUROPE ASIA
www.ccl.org

Published by Jossey-Bass
A Wiley Imprint
989 Market Street, San Francisco, CA 94103-1741   www.josseybass.com

Jossey-Bass books and products are available through most bookstores. To contact Jossey-Bass directly call our Customer Care Department within the U.S. at 800-956-7739, outside the U.S. at 317-572-3986, or fax 317-572-4002.

Jossey-Bass also publishes its books in a variety of electronic formats. Some content that appears in print may not be available in electronic books.

Library of Congress Cataloging-in-Publication Data

Hughes, Richard L.
  Becoming a strategic leader : your role in your organization's enduring success / by Richard L. Hughes, Katherine Colarelli Beatty.
      p. cm.—(Jossey-Bass business & management series)
  Includes bibliographical references and index.
  ISBN 0-7879-6867-6 (alk. paper)
  1. Leadership. 2. Strategic planning. 3. Organizational effectiveness. 4. Success in business. I. Beatty, Katherine Colarelli, 1965- II. Title. III. Series.
  HD57.7.H84 2005
  658.4'092—dc22   2004025830

Printed in the United States of America
FIRST EDITION
HB Printing   10 9 8 7 6 5

A Joint Publication of

The Jossey-Bass

Business & Management Series

and

The Center for Creative Leadership

Contents

Preface

We've worked together for eight years at the Center for Creative Leadership, and the focus of our work has been developing the strategic leadership of individual executives and their teams. During that time we have worked personally with nearly a thousand different managers and executives—sometimes with heterogeneous groups from different companies, and sometimes with groups from the same company.

Most often, that work has been in the context of a program called Developing the Strategic Leader (DSL). We've had the opportunity to work with the DSL executives as they've struggled to become better strategic leaders. Weathering this challenge alongside them has deepened our own understanding about how to become more strategic. In a general sense, this book reflects our attempt to put some of the lessons of that program and what we have learned through our work in it into a more explicit and accessible format.

One thing we have gained from this work is greater clarity about the challenges managers and executives face in becoming more effective strategic leaders. Our understanding has come in part from what executives themselves tell us about their challenges, which typically fall into the following broad categories: influencing others more effectively, particularly upwardly and outwardly; thinking strategically; achieving a better balance in handling short-term and long-term pressures; moving from a functional or departmental perspective to a broader organizational perspective; and actually creating or influencing organizational strategy.

Another thing we've gained from this work is an appreciation of how the nature of strategic leadership in organizations is changing, which is reflected in the people who describe these challenges to us. Specifically, we are finding that managers and executives at many levels and across many functions are signing up to improve their effectiveness as strategic leaders. For example, only about 8 percent of DSL participants represent the top leadership of their organizations; 48 percent are executives, 39 percent are from upper-middle management, and 5 percent are from middle management.

What does it mean to find such a broad spectrum of managers and executives intent on developing their effectiveness as strategic leaders? We believe it's more than just proactive preparation for future responsibilities. We believe it reflects something fundamental about how strategic leadership itself is changing—that strategic leadership is now the responsibility of many people, not just those at the top.

The challenges we discuss represent what managers and executives are struggling with now, not theoretical challenges they might confront in the future. In that regard, the list presents to us a fairly reasonable outline of what it means to be strategic. True, it is only a rather sparse outline. An important part of what we have learned over the years is how to help managers and executives add depth as well as breadth to this outline, in ways tailored to their unique development needs and circumstances. We've also learned a lot about what facilitates the development of strategic leadership, especially how the understanding and practice of strategic leadership evolves in an environment that plays host to an ongoing interplay of action, observation, and reflection.

Over time, we have also come to appreciate a certain connectedness between the kinds of experiences that facilitate the development of strategic leadership and those that facilitate the ongoing development, implementation, and refinement of organizational strategy itself. Both have everything to do with viewing strategy as a learning process, an idea that is central to this book. Part of becoming an effective strategic leader involves facilitating that process throughout the organization (or one's part of it).

Our title, *Becoming a Strategic Leader,* underscores a central lesson we've learned in this work: that strategic leadership is about *becoming.* It's about a process of never-ending individual, team, and organizational learning. Working at CCL and with the DSL program has been a privilege, in particular because of the opportunity we have had to help so many individuals play a more effective role in the strategic leadership of their organizations. We hope our insights from that work, captured here as best we can, will help them continue that process—and will reach new audiences as well.

Colorado Springs, Colorado   Richard L. Hughes
December 2004   Katherine Colarelli Beatty

Acknowledgments

This book represents the contributions of many people over many years, and we'd like to acknowledge our debt to them here.

Our ideas about strategic leadership have been largely formulated in the context of our work in CCL's Developing the Strategic Leader (DSL) program. We've learned much from executives participating in the program, and we've learned equally from our colleagues on the DSL faculty, who have enriched our understanding of the nature of strategic leadership. We are particularly indebted to fellow faculty members Kevin Asbjörnson, Stephanie Trovas, Laura Quinn, Pam Shipp, Ted Grubb, Dennis Lindoerfer, Gary Rhodes, Bruce Byington, Jessica Baltes, and Chuck Hinkle for their insight, savvy, generosity, and comradeship.

Some of our colleagues contributed in unique ways. Bruce Byington was an indispensable collaborator in helping us formulate and refine our understanding of strategy as a learning process, the framework on which this book is based. Jessica Baltes had many responsibilities in the DSL program, including an invaluable role in guiding the DSL research effort cited throughout the book. Judith Steed, Dennis Lindoerfer, Laura Quinn, and Cory Stern also helped significantly in the DSL research effort.

We are indebted to John McGuire for his contributions to our appreciating the role of culture in leadership strategy. We are indebted to Patricia O'Connor, Jennifer Martineau, and Davida Sharpe, whose impressive work with Catholic Healthcare Partners is highlighted in several chapters. Chuck Palus and David Horth's work on creative competencies had a significant impact on our own approach to strategic thinking. Sara King's and Bill Drath's support for the book took many forms, not the least of which was their continuing personal and institutional encouragement for the project.

We owe a particular debt of gratitude to Marcia Horowitz, who first suggested to us that our experiences in the DSL program be translated into a book. In that journey we could not have had more supportive or able collaborators than Peter Scisco, our editor, and Martin Wilcox, the director of CCL's Publications Group. We have been equally fortunate to work with the professionals at Jossey-Bass, notably Kathe Sweeney, Byron Schneider, and Tamara Keller.

Many organizations and many individuals are featured in stories throughout the book. We are grateful to those organizations for the opportunity to mention them here and to those individuals for sharing their experiences so generously and publicly. The organizations include Torstar, Harlequin, the *Toronto Star,* Verizon, Starbucks, Xerox, American Power Conversion, Neoforma, and Catholic Healthcare Partners. Those individuals include Rob Prichard, Karen Hanna, and Kim Eckel at Torstar; Donna Hayes, Trish Hewitt, and Isabel Swift at Harlequin; Marilyn O'Connell at Verizon; Margaret Wheeler at Starbucks; Tim Conlon and Jim Firestone at Xerox; Andrew Cole at American Power Conversion; Steve Wigginton, Rebecca Oles, and Amanda Mogin at Neoforma; and Jon Abeles at Catholic Healthcare Partners.

Several individuals gave us useful and detailed feedback on earlier drafts of the book, including Mark Edwards, Amy Edmondson, Bill Clover, and Nick Colarelli (Kate's dad).

We're particularly grateful for the help of Linda Hunter and Carol Vallee, who have supported this effort administratively during its development. Their creativity, patience, good humor, and attention to quality have made all the difference.

Finally, our deepest appreciation goes to those closest in our lives, whose understanding and support made our work on this long project possible: Chris, Mark, and Thomas Beatty, and Georgeann Hughes. You're the best!

The Authors

Richard L. Hughes (Rich) is a senior enterprise associate at the Center for Creative Leadership (CCL). His work focuses on studying the effectiveness of senior executives and their teams and developing their impact on organizations. Rich developed the Strategic Team Review and Action Tool (STRAT), an assessment used to provide feedback to executive teams on their effectiveness in handling strategic responsibilities. He spearheaded the development of CCL's architecture of strategic goals and objectives and its strategic scorecard. He joined the CCL staff in 1995 after serving ten years as a full professor and head of the Department of Behavioral Sciences and Leadership at the U.S. Air Force Academy. While there he was the principal architect of the Academy's plans for assessing and improving its educational effectiveness. Rich is the lead author of *Leadership: Enhancing the Lessons of Experience*, published by Irwin/McGraw-Hill. He received his B.S. from the U.S. Air Force Academy and his M.A. from the University of Texas. He holds a Ph.D. in clinical psychology from the University of Wyoming.

Katherine Colarelli Beatty (Kate) is the open-enrollment group manager for CCL's Leading Teams and Organizations group. Her responsibilities include directing training programs to create positive impact on individuals, teams, and organizations. Kate's expertise in strategic leadership is reflected in her many research, writing, public speaking, and training activities. She joined CCL in 1996. Prior to that she was a consultant to organizations in the areas of change, leadership, and team development. She also worked for Anheuser-Busch in its efforts to develop future company leaders, and she was a member of a leadership development program for engineers at GE Medical Systems. Kate earned her B.S. in electrical engineering at the University of Illinois. She holds M.S. and Ph.D. degrees in organizational psychology from Saint Louis University.

Introduction

What if you could turn your organization into an engine of sustained competitive advantage, with the agility to weather uncertainty and success with equal measure? What if you could transform your personal and technical skills into a leadership practice with the power to build an organization capable of ever-deepening insight and high performance?

What if you could have strategic leadership throughout your organization?

This book is your guide.

Strategic Leadership Is Your Responsibility

Have you noticed how it seems more difficult to get work done in organizations today? Do you need to interact with more and more people inside and outside your organization in order to be successful? Garnering resources for a project, for example, now often requires conversations and coordination among parties that did not have to interact before. In general, work has become more complex and more interdependent in most organizations.

How did this happen? It is the result of many factors that are probably familiar to you.

- *Pace of change:* CEOs are turning over faster, new products are being developed faster, new competitors are springing up faster, more and more regulatory requirements are being introduced—change keeps coming.

- *Increasing uncertainty:* Long-term forecasting and planning has become increasingly difficult and risky, if not impossible.

- *Growing ambiguity:* More and more problems confronting organizations are ill-defined and resistant to routine solutions.

- *Increasing complexity:* The problems people face today seem more complex than ever before. At the very least, the amount of information people must sift through to do their work grows daily, and more diverse perspectives are brought to bear on issues than ever before.

Changes like these have created a new competitive environment that has led to more complex and interdependent work in organizations and that also requires those same organizations to be more agile and resilient. Being both agile and resilient at the same time is not easy.

As a result, organizations may find themselves mistakenly trying to be all things to all people as they strive to meet these seemingly competing sets of external and internal demands. It becomes increasingly difficult to create focus in an organization and to harness that focus throughout the organization as tension between the internal needs and the external needs increases.

Paradoxically, this situation calls for more people in organizations to be engaged in strategic leadership, not fewer. To be sure, certain individuals have greater opportunity and responsibility to affect their organization than others. But more and more, people at all organizational levels and in all organizational functions are seeing opportunities to work in ways that affect the direction and momentum of the whole organization.

The best way for organizations to thrive in the face of this new reality is to become continual learning engines. In practical terms, that means that organizational strategy—the vision, the directions, and the tactics adopted to move toward success—ought to be held in an ongoing state of formulation, implementation, reassessment, and revision. We more fully illustrate and explore the implications of that statement in Chapter One, but by way of introduction consider the view that organizational strategy is a learning process that includes five elements:

- *Assessing where we are:* This relates to collecting information about and making sense of the organization's competitive environment.
- *Understanding who we are and where we want to go:* This refers to the organization's aspirations, including its vision, mission, and core values.
- *Learning how to get there:* This is the formulation of strategy, including determination of priorities.
- *Making the journey:* This involves translating the strategy into action by identifying and implementing tactics.
- *Checking our progress:* This is the continuing assessment of the organization's effectiveness, leading then to a reassessment at the organization's new level of performance, which it has achieved through the other elements. This starts the learning process all over again.

The leadership required for organizations during this process must align vision, resources, and commitment so that the organization maintains forward momentum in the midst of change.

So what kind of leadership meets those requirements? It is the kind that makes decisions and takes action not just to boost the organization's current performance but also to strengthen its future effectiveness and competitiveness. It's not the kind of leadership that can be explained and practiced with a simple set of procedures ("how to do strategic planning," for example). Instead, individuals propel their organization through successive iterations of this learning process with strategic thinking, strategic acting, and strategic influencing skills. These skills are needed in every element of the learning process and can be practiced by leaders at every level in the organization. They create fuel to drive the organization's learning process and to link it to the organization's evolving strategic intent for creating and sustaining competitive advantage. Taken together, they constitute strategic leadership.

In this book we will show you how to develop and to practice leadership skills with strategic intent. We show you how to form a nucleus of vision and action and how to spread that energy to others so that it multiplies and intensifies. In the process you and others will transform your organization into a learning engine that is adaptable, flexible, and resilient.

The Contents of This Book

Our book describes a comprehensive conceptual framework to help you understand this view of strategic leadership. It also presents practical suggestions about how to develop such leadership.

In Chapter One we address the unique nature of strategic leadership and what makes it so difficult and challenging. We examine in some depth the idea of organizational strategy as a learning process and conclude by looking at the implications of adopting that view.

Strategic thinking, the subject of Chapter Two, refers to the cognitive dimension of strategic leadership. This aspect might include, for example, discerning environmental trends that have strategic significance for your organization. It might also include the ability to sift through waves of information to identify the most strategically significant facts or issues. Other aspects include seeing things from an enterprise perspective, appreciating how all the different functions and departments in the organization contribute to an integrated whole, and looking at things in new and different ways.

Chapter Three takes up the mantle of strategic acting, the behavioral dimension of strategic leadership. The importance of acting with strategic intent can't be overstated. Ultimately, everything comes down to what a leader does or doesn't do. Great vision and detailed plans amount to nothing if they aren't carried out with purpose. Not even the sharpest insight has value unless it leads to decisions that commit resources toward certain activities rather than others.

Strategic influencing is the subject of Chapter Four. It refers to the ways in which leaders influence others and the ways they open themselves up to influence from others. Influence is the channel through which thought and action flow throughout the organization. It's critical to maintaining positive traction along the organization's strategic path.

Because organizations depend not just on individual effort but on the effort of individuals working together—often on teams—we use Chapter Five to examine the nature and effectiveness of collaborative strategic leadership. We draw heavily upon research that we have conducted on teams in the context of CCL's Developing the Strategic Leader (DSL) program.

Individuals and teams enact strategic leadership when they think, act, and influence others in ways that enhance the organization's sustainable competitive advantage. But what kinds of conditions in organizations are most likely to encourage individuals and teams to develop and practice leadership in this way? Chapter Six describes that kind of environment. It looks at the aspects of organizational culture, structure, and systems most likely to produce and support the kind of leadership that will keep organizations moving forward along a path of continual learning.

In Chapter Seven we return to a more personal focus and offer a few final suggestions about how readers can best develop their own strategic leader capabilities. Those efforts revolve around choosing experiences rich in learning opportunities.

The Audience for This Book

Our premise is that strategic leadership is a process, not a position, and increasing numbers of individuals share in the responsibility of its development and practice in organizations. That shared responsibility even extends to certain aspects of creating strategy and is not limited to just executing a strategy passed down from above. Furthermore, certain teams as well as individuals exert strategic leadership in their organizations, reflecting the increasingly collaborative nature of this process. More than any other organizational activity, it represents the confluence of ideas and action. We've said many times in our DSL program that strategic leadership exists in the white spaces on organizational charts. No single functional area or group has the breadth of information and perspective necessary to effectively guide an organization through the learning process that brings sustained competitive advantage.

With that view in mind, we believe that this book offers somewhat distinctive benefits to three different groups: younger or junior managers, middle managers, and executives.

For younger or junior managers, the book is an introduction to the basic concepts of strategy and strategic leadership. It demystifies and makes relevant concepts that otherwise may sound confusing or irrelevant to one's role in the organization.

The book will also be helpful for middle managers. By definition they link levels above and below them, so middle managers are critical to assuring that strategy is both a top-down and a bottom-up process. Increasingly, we find, strategic leadership has a "middle-out" dimension to it. The book suggests many ways of influencing the whole organization from positions other than the top.

Executives may have the best vantage point from which to affect the quality of strategic leadership throughout the whole organization. They have responsibility for bringing information into the organization and for making the furthest-reaching decisions, and they have the opportunity to create the necessary momentum among their peers, direct reports, and even their bosses. It's that energy that can transform an organization by bringing it full awareness of its circumstances and challenges, and that enables it to remain flexible, creative, adaptive, forward-looking, and strategic in its intent. Those are the qualities of sustained competitive advantage, the goal of every strategic leader. The parts of the book dealing with how to create organizational conditions that encourage effective strategic leadership by individuals and teams will be especially useful to executives.

Chapter One

What Is Strategic Leadership?

Imagine that you are standing on a beautiful beach, with the sand between your toes, looking out over the deep blue-green water. You feel a fresh and invigorating breeze on your face. You hear the roar of waves breaking in the distance. Every once in a while your warm feet feel the relief of cool water when a particularly strong wave makes its way up the beach.

Your watching the ocean has a purpose, for you have a surfboard in hand. You've practiced at home: lying on your board in your living room and working to pop up to your feet in a quick and flowing motion. You've practiced with small waves: picking those big enough to pick you up, but not big enough to toss you over.

Now you want to try your luck on the bigger waves. You walk into the water, get on your surfboard, and paddle out to where the waves are breaking. The wind is strong today, and the waves are big. As you reach what appears to be the best spot, waves are crashing around you and you are tossed about in the water. You try to catch a wave, turning the nose of your surfboard toward the beach and popping up to your feet on the board, but your timing is off and you find yourself back in the water with the wave and your surfboard crashing over you. You try again, and this time you make it to your feet, but as you stand up you lose your balance and fall. You try again, but are unable to catch the next wave as it rapidly passes by you. Attempt after attempt is met with sour results. You try to figure out what is going wrong, but waves are passing you by and your day of beautiful surfing is turning into a day of frustration. Paddling back to shore, you are not sure what you did wrong, but you hope that the next time will produce a different result.

Now imagine yourself at work. You've worked hard for a number of years and been rewarded with several promotions. But you've recently learned from your boss that, while the organization values your operational leadership skills, people do not view you as a strategic leader. You asked your boss what that means, only to receive a shrug and "You know, be strategic" in reply. You've looked to others to help you understand this feedback, but people seem unable to explain what "being strategic" really means. Just as it's difficult to learn to surf when you don't know what you're doing wrong, it's also difficult to become strategic when you don't understand how you are not that way now and people cannot tell you what to do differently.

Increasingly, organizations are calling on people at all levels to be strategic. Even if you have not heard that you need to be more strategic, we bet you can think of others with whom you work who need to develop their strategic capabilities. However, the path to that end is neither clear nor well defined. In some ways, it may feel a bit like learning to surf. You find yourself in the middle of chaos, business issues and initiatives swirling all around you like waves. You're not quite sure which one calls for your best energies (which waves to catch), and even if you pick one you might not be able to find your balance and ride it to a satisfactory conclusion.

Our intent in this book is to help you become strategic. We also intend to help you help others throughout your organization become more strategic and to help teams with strategic responsibilities to meet those demands more effectively. In this chapter we'll lay a foundation by exploring the nature of strategic leadership and the nature of strategy making as we consider the following questions:

- What are the definition and focus of strategic leadership?
- How does strategic leadership differ from leadership?
- What makes strategic leadership so difficult and challenging?

- How can strategy-making and strategy-implementing processes work in organizations to create enduring success?
- What are the implications for leaders of making and implementing strategy?

With this groundwork in place, then, we will turn our attention in successive chapters to the specific question of *how* individuals and teams exercise strategic leadership.

The Definition and Focus of Strategic Leadership

Individuals and teams enact strategic leadership when they think, act, and influence in ways that promote the sustainable competitive advantage of the organization.

This statement is a real mouthful. But because it encompasses all of the critical elements of strategic leadership, we offer it as our definition.

The focus of strategic leadership is sustainable competitive advantage, or the enduring success of the organization. Indeed, this is the work of strategic leadership: to drive and move an organization so that it will thrive in the long term. This is true whether the organization is for-profit or nonprofit. It depends only on whether your organization seeks and achieves an enduring set of capabilities that provide distinctive value to stakeholders over the long term, in whatever sector your organization operates or whatever bottom line you are measured by.

Later in this chapter, we'll discuss the strategy process in more detail and how it can be used to help create sustainable competitive advantage. But for now, let's explore leadership that creates sustainable competitive advantage by considering two organizations: IBM and Digital Equipment Corporation.

IBM

In 1993, many experts in the technology industries had concluded that IBM was inching toward its last days as an organization. Although the company had its most profitable year in 1990, the early

1990s saw big changes in the world of computers. Smaller, more nimble companies were innovating their way into the hearts of consumers and businesses, and the traditional big computers produced by IBM were seen as outdated, old technology. IBM stock had dropped from its 1987 high of $43 a share to less than $13 a share at the end of the first quarter of 1993 (Gerstner, 2002). Lou Gerstner joined IBM as its CEO in April 1993. IBM was on the verge of being split into autonomous business units when Gerstner arrived, a move that would have dissolved the organization that had long been a computer industry icon.

Gerstner chose a different path for the company. He kept the company together and took critical and bold steps not only to keep the company alive but to revitalize it to the point where it again led the industry. Most notably, Gerstner adopted a new strategy that moved the company from a product-driven approach to a service-driven approach. This was no easy task. It required a complete retooling of the people, processes, and systems in the organization. But the work paid off, and IBM's stock rose every year except one until Gerstner retired early in 2002.

Digital Equipment Corporation

Contrast IBM's story with the story of one of its key competitors, Digital Equipment Corporation (DEC; see Digital Equipment Corporation, 2004, paragraph 3). Ken Olsen founded DEC in 1957 and ran the company until the 1990s, when Robert Palmer replaced him. DEC was known for several advances in the computer industry, including the first commercially viable minicomputer and the first laptop. Additionally, it was the first commercial business connected to the Internet.

With more than a hundred thousand employees, DEC was the second-largest computer company in the world at its peak in the late 1980s. But it does not exist as an organization today. With the successes of the 1980s, the company became more and more insular. Products were well designed, but they would work only with other

DEC products and so customers tended to overlook them. Ken Olsen also believed that superiorly engineered products would stand alone and did not need advertising. When the new RA-90 disk drive came to market very late and several other products ran into trouble, competitors overtook the company with similar products at lower prices. DEC experienced its first layoffs in the early 1990s. The company was sold to Compaq in 1998, and then Hewlett-Packard acquired Compaq in 2002. Clearly DEC was led with great fervor and the company was able to achieve great things. But that greatness was not sustained.

What Makes Strategic Leadership Different?

What led IBM to thrive, but DEC to die? Why was IBM able to weather a very difficult storm, make necessary changes, embark on a new path, and reach success in a new way, while DEC was swallowed up by its competition? The short answer is that effective strategic leadership—leadership focused on sustainable competitive advantage—was enacted at IBM.

When we discuss sustainable competitive advantage as the focus of strategic leadership, some of the executives we work with ask us, "Isn't that just leadership? How are they different? If you're a good leader, why aren't you, by definition, a good strategic leader?" That is not an easy question to answer, but our research and experience reveal some subtle and important differences: strategic leadership is exerted when the decisions and actions of leaders have strategic implications for the organization. It might also be described in this way:

- Strategic leadership is broad in scope.
- The impact of strategic leadership is felt over long periods of time.
- Strategic leadership often involves significant organizational change.

Scope

The broad scope of strategic leadership means that it impacts areas outside the leader's own functional area and business unit—and even outside the organization. This broad scope requires seeing the organization as an interdependent and interconnected system of multiple parts, where decisions in one area provoke actions in other areas. The waves in our surfer's ocean provide an analogy: As each wave crashes to the surface it disturbs the water, which moves in reaction to the falling wave. External forces, such as the wind, also affect the waves. In the same way, the scope of strategic leadership extends beyond the organization, acting on and reacting to trends and issues in the environment.

The scope of leadership does not necessarily extend this far. For example, a person who facilitates the decision-making process of a group demonstrates effective leadership even if the decision is small in scope, such as assigning group members to parts of a project.

Duration

Like its scope, the time frame of strategic leadership is also far-reaching. The strategic leader must keep long-term goals in mind while working to achieve short-term objectives. Nearly half a millennium ago, the Japanese military leader Miyamoto Musashi said, "In strategy, it is important to see distant things as if they were close and to take a distanced view of close things" (Advice on Strategy, n.d.). His apt observation describes the tension between short-term and long-term perspectives that strategic leaders must balance.

In contrast, not all leadership requires this forward view to be effective. Very good operational leaders manage day-to-day functions effectively and are skilled at working with people to ensure that short-term objectives are met. This is important work, but it does not always need to take the long term into account.

Organizational Change

A third way strategic leadership differs from leadership in general is that it results in significant change. For example, consider the strategic impact of a new compensation system that touches all parts of the organization, provides a structure for defining differences in roles and appropriate salary ranges, and ties performance plans and measures to the strategic objectives of the organization, giving people a clear understanding of what is required to advance along various career ladders. The human resources team that designed and implemented this system, replacing one that included no common understanding of appropriate salary ranges for roles, criteria for raises, and career progression, exercised genuine strategic leadership.

Effective leadership does not necessarily institute significant organizational change. Leading a team to complete a recurring task, such as closing out the quarterly books for the organization, is an example of effective leadership that does not create significant change.

Leadership, Not Strategic Leadership

To further explore the specific meaning of strategic leadership, let's look at two critical and important leadership behaviors that do not involve strategic implications.

Coaching a direct report is one example. As you make the transition from individual contributor to managing and leading others, getting results through others rather than through your own direct efforts is a critical leadership skill. Coaching may involve structuring assignments, motivating and supporting the development of the person, and challenging the person to think about things in different ways. While coaching a direct report can have a profound impact on that individual in the long run, it does not necessarily have strategic implications. However, developing an organizational priority and system to ensure that everyone receives effective coaching does have strategic implications.

Another example of leadership that does not have strategic implications is leading a team to complete a task that is not strategic in nature. A team assigned to open up a new retail outlet store in a global company that has thousands of such stores worldwide is a case in point. The team may consist of several members whose collective goal is to open the new store in a timely and effective way. Such a setup team will move from one store opening to the next. Although this work is absolutely critical to the successful implementation of the organization's overall strategy, it is not in and of itself strategic in nature. The scope and time frame are not far-reaching, nor does this work involve significant organizational change. However, if members of this team work with others to review the distribution of stores across the world, to understand trends among consumers, and to create plans for new store openings and closures, then that work would have strategic implications.

Where Strategic Leadership Falters

Creating sustainable competitive advantage for an organization is no easy task. It requires bright and capable people, but that is not enough. For example, the employees of Digital Equipment Corporation were smart enough to develop new technologies that pushed the technology industry forward. The individuals who ran IBM before Gerstner arrived were also bright—in fact, he was taken aback by the potential and capabilities of the people he met when he arrived there: "How could such truly talented people allow themselves to get into such a morass?" (Gerstner, 2002, p. 42). If the level of intelligence among its workforce did not differentiate IBM from DEC, then what did? What keeps organizations and their leaders from being successfully strategic? Frequently, the obstacles fall into three categories:

- *Lack of focus:* Organizations and the leaders in them try to be all things to all people, and they fail to make the tough decisions that provide a strategic focus.

- *Loose tactics:* The things that people, departments, and functional areas actually do are not aligned with the organization's strategy.
- *Limited range:* Leaders focus on short-term success at the expense of long-term viability.

Lack of Focus

An ill-defined or undefined strategy indicates that an organization has not made difficult but necessary choices. As Michael Porter of the Harvard Business School has said, "Strategy renders choices about what not to do as important as choices about what to do" (Porter, 1996, p. 77). Information collected from strategic leadership teams as part of CCL's Developing the Strategic Leader (DSL) program indicates that it is rare for organizations to have a strategy that is discriminating (clear about what will be done and what will not be done). This is particularly true in organizations that adopt strategies to copy their competitors. Avoiding difficult choices and refusing to discriminate can lead to a kitchen-sink strategy—one that includes a little bit of everything, the opposite of focus.

In an informal poll of the readers of one of CCL's electronic publications, 35 percent of the respondents said that lack of clarity about organizational strategy hinders their ability to be strategic (Beatty, 2003). Additionally, CFO *Magazine* found similar results in one of its polls (Lazere, 1998), where lack of a well-defined strategy was the most frequent (57 percent) explanation for a lack of value in the planning process.

A lack of focus affects people in organizations by making them feel overly pressured for time and overcommitted. They do not have a sense of what can come off their plates. The executives participating in our DSL program frequently mention that lack of time is one of their personal challenges to being more strategic. Additionally, a lack of common understanding about the strategy allows personal agendas to form and be pursued. Politics runs rampant as individuals try to look good against criteria that they have developed without having reached consensus across the organization that those criteria are indeed the right ones for measuring success.

Loose Tactics

Even with a common understanding of the strategy, actually making choices that are consistent with that understanding is hard to do. A strategic plan itself is only a plan; an organization's actual strategy lies in the decisions and choices its members make as they enact, or fail to enact, the plan.

A study by Benchmarking Solutions (cited in Banham, 1999) found that only 27 percent of companies fully integrate their tactics and strategies. More companies (58 percent) have some form of integration at the highest level, but transferring that integration to lower levels does not often happen.

Tactics may also be misaligned because people throughout the organization don't really understand what the strategy means for them on a day-to-day basis. Information collected from strategic leadership teams we have worked with supports the notion that individuals at all levels of their organization rarely understand how their roles support the organization's mission and strategy. In some cases this is because the strategy does not create focus. But in other cases, formal and coordinated communication systems are ineffective or nonexistent, so people get mixed messages about the strategy. A Watson-Wyatt survey of 293 organizations in the United Kingdom (Stewart, 1999) found that 67 percent of employees in well-performing organizations have a good understanding of their overall organizational goals, whereas only 38 percent do in poorly performing organizations. Further, the survey revealed that in all organizations communication could be significantly improved.

Limited Range

Many of our DSL executives feel a tremendous pressure to make short-term numbers. In fact, it is the most frequently mentioned issue when we ask them to define the major personal challenge to their becoming strategic leaders. For example, one executive characterized the challenge as "Balancing current operational needs versus looking at the long-term perspective of growth and development of our staff and business practice." Another said, "I need to let go of the busy day-to-day activities and spend more time thinking about the future."

In our experience, such executives have typically risen through the ranks by being rewarded for their strong operational leadership, their ability to fight the daily fires and come out ahead. (In fact, one executive commented that he was so good at fighting fires that he sometimes created them just so that he could fight them.) When a person has developed such strength in a particular area, it is very difficult for that person to shift focus and do something different. When it comes to developing the capacity for strategic leadership, it is extremely challenging for executives to let go of the day-to-day issues, even if they are potentially in conflict with the long-term issues.

Lou Gerstner provides a potent example of someone who was able to make a decision for the long run, even though it clearly had negative short-term implications. When he took over IBM in 1993, the company was bleeding cash. Mainframe revenue had fallen from $13 billion in 1990 to around $7 billion in 1993, and competitors were slashing mainframe prices to levels significantly below the prices of IBM products. Customers were asking IBM to do the same, so keeping prices above the competition ran the long-term risk of losing key customers. However, cutting prices would further threaten IBM's cash position in the short term. Gerstner chose to slash prices, and he believes this was one of the key decisions to saving IBM (2002, pp. 44–48).

Clearly the line between meeting short-term operational pressures and long-term success is a difficult one to walk, particularly for publicly traded companies that are under Wall Street's daily microscope. For these organizations, balancing the pressure of Wall Street is critical not only in the short run but also over the long run, because significant and sustained drops in stock price can have tremendous long-term impact. We are not saying that short-term success is not important. But when an organization consistently favors the short term over the long term by, for example, neglecting to make investments to keep resources and technology up-to-date, the organization will suffer in the end.

The Work of the Strategic Leader

These challenges to strategic leadership—the challenge to create focus, the challenge to align tactics with strategy, and the challenge to keep the long term in mind despite short-term pressures—are not surprising given the kind of environment organizations currently operate in. An increasing pace of change and growing uncertainty and ambiguity define that world. As a result of organizations' efforts to thrive in this environment, the world of work has become more complex and interdependent; just think of the complex organizational structures, systems, and processes that exist today to deal with this environment. Now also consider the fact that, amid this complexity and interdependence, organizations must also be resilient and flexible to continue to thrive.

Creating a sustainable competitive advantage is no easy task. It involves bridging the gap between internal complexity and interdependence on one hand and the need for flexibility and resilience on the other. Balancing this tension is the work of the strategic leader.

Creating Sustainability

By "creating sustainable competitive advantage," we mean that strategic leaders work toward a future state of enhanced vitality for their organization so that it will endure in the long term. Therefore, they are clearly implementing changes to the organization. But it is more than just change after change. The critical issue for strategic leaders is how to make changes that progressively build on each other. The right changes represent an evolving enhancement of the organization's vitality. They are changes that help an organization endure in the midst of a dynamic environment, not changes that sap energy and that, cumulatively, don't reflect developing capabilities and value.

Imagine yourself again as the surfer we described at the beginning of this chapter. Remember how, when going for a big wave for the first time, you made changes to your approach by pointing your board in a slightly different direction, changing the timing of your standing up on the board, making subtle changes to your weight distribution to keep your balance, and trying to catch waves at different points relative to their crest. But your changes had little impact because you did not understand the underlying issues that were keeping you from success. You just kept trying whatever came to mind, without stopping to reflect and learn from each of your attempts.

Leading an organization is clearly more difficult than surfing, but both require learning. Successfully creating sustainability through changes that progressively build on each other requires a learning engine that runs throughout the organization. Strategy-making and strategy-implementation processes provide the foundation for that learning engine, and strategic leadership is what drives it. We use a framework called "strategy as a learning process" to depict this engine. It describes a specific strategy mind-set, a way of thinking about how to craft and implement strategy. In particular, it implies that successful strategy operates in an ongoing state of formulation, implementation, reassessment, and revision. Let's briefly introduce the concept here, and then deepen our understanding by showing how it has played out in one company, Neoforma.

The Learning Process

Organizations and their leaders have certain theories about what will lead to success in their industries. They test these theories through the actions and decisions they make. They watch key indicators to see how they are doing. If the key indicators are as they expect, executives consider the organization to be on track. If the indicators reveal unexpected results, leaders will typically make changes. During the course of this work, a process of learning is taking place.

This process has five primary elements, as depicted in Figure 1.1.

Figure 1.1. Strategy as a Learning Process: Overview.

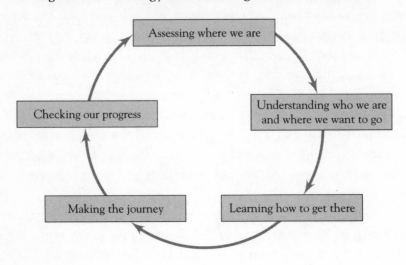

- *Assessing where we are* refers to the process of collecting relevant information and making sense of the organization's competitive environment.
- *Understanding who we are and where we want to go* refers to the aspirational dimension of organizational strategy, including the organization's vision, mission, and core values.
- *Learning how to get there* involves understanding and formulating the critical elements of strategy.
- *Making the journey* involves translating the strategy into action by identifying and implementing tactics.
- *Checking our progress* is the continuing assessment of effectiveness. This part then leads to a reassessment at the organization's new level of performance, starting the learning cycle over again.

As illustrated in Figure 1.1, learning in organizations occurs as a cycle. Organizations go through life phases, which may be difficult to differentiate in the moment but often can be used in hindsight to describe the organization's evolution and growth. Neoforma, which provides supply chain management solutions to health care organizations, vividly illustrates this cycle. Its evolutionary phases build upon each other, progressively enhancing its vitality.

Neoforma's Journey

Throughout its life, Neoforma has focused on how technology can be used to support business practices in health care. People who specialized in architecture and physics founded the company in 1996, and their first product was a CD that was used to provide guidance for building medical rooms and facilities. The organization has grown and changed over the years. At the time of this publication, it has moved from helping build medical facilities to supporting approximately $8 billion in health care purchasing annually. The following sections explore its evolution in more detail.

Phase One: Technology.   Neoforma was founded during the growth of the Internet, so not surprisingly the company fairly quickly moved to a Web-based product. Building upon the founders' ideas, the new Web-based product combined the planning and guidance functions of the CD with a public marketplace to buy medical supplies and auction used medical equipment. As its business grew, Neoforma's executives began to understand the potential of the marketplace functions of their product and to recognize the role of the Internet in achieving that potential. They saw that, as a supply chain management solution, the Internet could save hospitals and suppliers billions of dollars by enabling effective collaboration between them. The Internet's ability to connect hospitals and their suppliers in a low-cost way was the key—in the eyes of Neoforma's leadership team—to its success. The prevailing belief was that introducing this technology would require significant changes on the part of the hospitals, but that the potential for cost reductions was so great that hospitals would tolerate the short-term disruption.

Unfortunately, this early theory that technology would prevail met a harsh reality. The way the Neoforma processes were designed (for the public marketplace) did not match the way hospitals purchased their supplies. They had their own legacy systems to track inventory and make purchases, and the assumption that the cost savings would override the difficulty of changing these systems just did not hold. Also, the price of the software and supporting services was high. While hospitals are generally open to spending money on technology that is directly related to clinical applications, they are very conservative outside those applications. In fact, the Neoforma executives discovered that hospitals typically invest less than 1 percent of their revenue in business information systems, compared to an average of 3 to 10 percent for the typical U.S. corporation. Further, suppliers were not attracted to a strategy of building a customer base one hospital at a time. Neoforma needed those suppliers if it was to manage the supply chain effectively.

As Neoforma executives struggled to understand their situation, they focused on how hospitals connected with their suppliers without the technology of the Internet. Specifically, they delved into the world of co-ops, organizations that facilitate connections of hospitals and suppliers to achieve economies of scale in supply costs. Novation is one such co-op. It was formed through an alliance between two major hospital systems and represents about two thousand hospitals, or one-third of the U.S. market. Neoforma executives learned that the business processes inherent to Novation's success were largely paper based.

Phase Two: Partnership. Around the year 2000, Neoforma executives saw the potential of a partnership with Novation. Neoforma's technology could be modified to create a private marketplace that matched the existing systems in the Novation hospitals. And this technology would facilitate the business relationships that Novation had already established. If Neoforma agreed to develop the technology of a private marketplace for Novation hospitals, it would receive the benefit of access to these hospitals, something that could fuel its growth tremendously. So its leaders agreed to this partnership and began the next phase of their journey.

During the transition to the partnership, Neoforma's focus and understanding of how it was going to be successful changed, from "selling our technology to hospitals one at a time" to "partnering with a key co-op to extend our reach in efficient ways." The leadership quickly oriented the entire company to delivering to its key customer, Novation. For example, a team was formed to digest the requirements and agreements created between Novation and the hospitals. Additionally, significant shifts were made to encourage a more customer-oriented culture within Neoforma, as opposed to the inward focus and individualism of the previous culture. For example, Neoforma's staff members had to learn and use the language of their customers, setting aside the technical language that had been the basis of their communication in the past.

Success came quickly to Neoforma through this strategy. Whereas 2001 adjusted revenues were approximately $28 million, 2002 adjusted revenues were $70 million. However, $70 million was the top of the best projection regarding success of the relationship with Novation. So the success raised the questions: What's next? How do we continue to grow?

In mid-2002, the Neoforma executives gathered in an off-site planning meeting. Naturally, questions were being asked about the next steps. There was no clear agreement. But a decision was made to shift focus again. Now that the company had established itself in the industry, it was time to reclaim the Neoforma brand.

Phase Three: Brand. In the course of a few months, creating brand awareness in non-Novation hospitals became a core focus. Essentially, Neoforma's entire product base had been branded under the Novation name. Questions such as these were raised: How do we extract the products under the brand? How do we inform the market, and talk about solutions versus marketplaces? (*Marketplaces* was Novation's term.) How do we describe who we are? What we do? What we care about?

As the changes were designed and implemented, the challenge of selling to one hospital at a time resurfaced. At this point, Neoforma executives understood the conservative nature of hospitals—specifically, the scarcity of "early adopters" when it comes to nonclinical applications. Most hospitals ask two questions when considering something new: Can you prove to me that it works? and Can you show me how the hospital benefits from it, given its unique aspects? Neoforma executives came to a deeper understanding of how important those questions were to creating credibility with new hospitals. They learned that they needed to demonstrate success in their installed base so that they could answer those questions for potential customers. In this third stage, their prevailing strategy changed to driving the adoption of and reliance on their solutions in their installed base.

Defining Strategy as a Learning Process

Neoforma's journey is similar to the journey that all organizations make. There is evolution, possibly even an occasional revolution, as the organization tries different approaches, learns from those attempts, and implements strategic change. Neoforma's journey has been a learning process much like the one depicted in Figure 1.1. But as we apply this concept to organizations, and specifically to how they craft and implement strategy, it requires adding more depth to our depiction of the process, as shown in Figure 1.2.

Assessing Where We Are.   Leading organizational learning requires assessing where it is now—that is, collecting and making sense of relevant information about the organization and its environment.

At different points in Neoforma's life cycle, a range of assessments was made about the state of the company in the industry. Diverse pieces of industry data became relevant at different times for the Neoforma leadership team. It learned about the state of technology in nonclinical applications in hospitals and the general nature of IT spending in hospitals. Neoforma executives also learned

Figure 1.2. Strategy as a Learning Process: Detail.

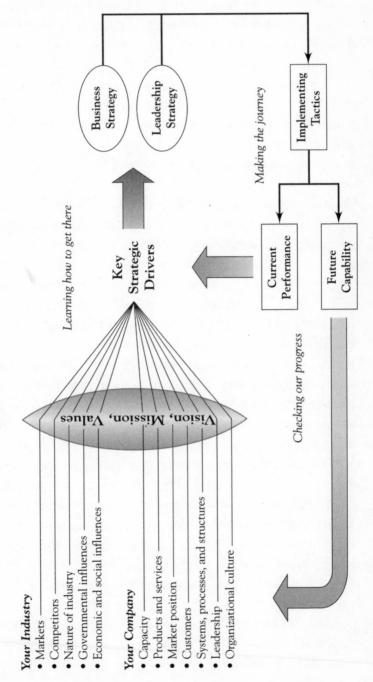

Assessing where we are

Understanding who we are and where we want to go

Learning how to get there

Your Industry
- Markets
- Competitors
- Nature of industry
- Governmental influences
- Economic and social influences

Your Company
- Capacity
- Products and services
- Market position
- Customers
- Systems, processes, and structures
- Leadership
- Organizational culture

Vision, Mission, Values

Key Strategic Drivers

Business Strategy

Leadership Strategy

Implementing Tactics

Making the journey

Current Performance

Future Capability

Checking our progress

more about the way in which hospitals work together to achieve efficiencies in purchasing, and the conservative, even skeptical, nature of hospital purchasing decisions. They also assessed the changing nature of their own industry as it consolidated (in 2000, Neoforma competed with nearly 150 different players; by the end of 2003, that field had narrowed to a single consortium of suppliers). Each lesson drawn from this information and analysis caused Neoforma's executive team to think differently about its own company—for example, the way in which it was structured and how it allocated resources.

Understanding Who We Are and Where We Want to Go. This part of the learning process refers to the aspirational aspects of strategy making, including vision, mission, and core values. Our placement of it in Figure 1.2 is meant to represent the idea that these elements of strategy create a lens through which internal and external conditions are understood and evaluated; they are not derived from internal or external conditions. What is the identity of the organization? In what ways does that identity shape organization members' views of what is possible or not possible? For example, does the organization's mission suggest that certain strategies should not be considered?

The identity of Neoforma was refined over the years. It continues to provide essentially the same services and products (other than facilities planning), but the way in which it provides services and products has changed. That change has affected the way in which it thinks of itself. It has moved from an organization totally focused on a key partnership to one that creates and markets a brand of products and services. To get a flavor of the change we are talking about, read these excerpts from the company description (on its Web site) as this description has evolved over the years:

> 1999: The company is transforming the healthcare industry by delivering information to the people who need it using the proven efficiencies of the Internet. [Phase One: Technology]

2000: Neoforma builds and operates leading Internet marketplaces that empower healthcare trading partners to optimize supply chain performance. [Phase Two: Partnership]

2003: Neoforma is a leading supply-chain management solutions provider for the healthcare industry. Through a unique combination of technology, information, and services, Neoforma provides innovative solutions to over 1,450 hospitals and suppliers, supporting more than $8 billion in annualized transaction volume. [Phase Three: Brand]

Learning How to Get There. This element, depicted in Figure 1.2, is critical to the learning-process framework. It includes a focus on key strategic drivers and the business and leadership strategies necessary to satisfy those drivers. Let's further explore these concepts and how Neoforma put them into action.

> *Strategic drivers* are those relatively few determinants of sustainable competitive advantage for a particular organization in a particular industry or competitive environment (also called factors of competitive success, key success factors, key value propositions).

Most organizations do not have more than three to five strategic drivers at any one time, and these invariably represent a subset of factors on which different companies in the industry compete. Organizations make choices about which strategic drivers they want to invest in—and excel at—in order to differentiate themselves in their industry. The reason for identifying a relatively small number of strategic drivers for your organization is primarily to ensure that you become focused about what pattern of inherently limited investments will give you the greatest strategic leverage and competitive advantage.

Drivers can change over time, or the relative emphasis on those drivers can change, as an organization satisfies its key driver. For example, in a high-growth industry, simply having available capacity may be the key driver of an organization. As the growth curve flattens, other competitive factors come into play.

In *learning how to get there*, organizations also employ (consciously or not) two types of strategies: business strategy and leadership strategy.

> *Business strategy* is the pattern of choices an organization
> makes to achieve sustainable competitive advantage.

Strategy involves a pattern of choices reflected in different parts of the business. For example, if being a high-quality provider is a critical element of an organization's strategy, then investments related to quality would be visible wherever you look: product design would include high-end features, manufacturing would ensure consistent production, customer service would be fully staffed with highly capable and knowledgeable people, the sales force would ensure a personal touch with customers, and so on.

In addition, strategy involves a series of choices. In order to dedicate more money to quality, the organization purposefully spends less money elsewhere. For example, it may realize that mass advertising does not play a role in its success, and so it limits expenditures there. Finally, the strategy must be linked to the key drivers to ensure sustainable competitive advantage.

> *Leadership strategy* describes the organizational and human
> capabilities needed to enact the business strategy effectively.

What type of culture should an organization engender to create success? What perspectives and abilities must individual leaders and teams have to be successful? What will they do to develop these skills and perspectives? Many organizations fail to pay attention to these "soft side" issues that are critical to success. The world of mergers and acquisitions provides a potent example of how inattention to the soft side can lead to failure. The statistics for mergers and acquisitions are sobering. Timothy Galpin and Mark Herndon (1999) note that 70 percent of merger and acquisition deals do not achieve their projected synergies, and they cite many studies showing that the primary issues in those failures are the people and organizational culture issues.

Neoforma has clearly tried different approaches to achieving success, some of which have worked better than others, and some of which worked for a time, but then changed in terms of priority. For example, its leaders quickly learned that their initial driver—a pure focus on technology—was important in the early stages, but was not going to lead them to success in the long term. Another driver became important as they learned more about their industry: marketing and distribution channels. Specifically, they needed to focus on how they reached their customer base and how they established credibility with that base. This is not to say that the technology was not important—it just was lower in terms of priority after Phase One.

During Phases Two and Three, the drivers have not changed. That is, in both phases the company is emphasizing the ways in which it reaches its customers and also the products it can deliver. However, the difference between Phases Two and Three lies in the strategies Neoforma adopted for reaching those customers. In Phase Two, the strategy was a partnership with Novation. In Phase Three, the strategy involved the adoption of and reliance on solutions in Neoforma's installed base to demonstrate both "proof" and "how" to potential customers.

Neoforma has also focused on the "soft side" of the business, although its executives would acknowledge that the leadership strategy has been less explicit than the business strategy. In the early days, its culture was focused inward and was individualistic; it rewarded those who succeeded in making technology better. As Neoforma came to understand the need for an emphasis on reaching its customers through marketing and distribution, the culture became much more customer focused. People learned to use the language of their customers (Novation's language in the partnership phase, and the end users' language in the brand phase) and to focus on the users' requirements.

Making the Journey. This part of the learning process framework involves translating the strategy into action by identifying and implementing tactics. In making the journey, Neoforma chose tactics consistent with its strategies. For example, during the technology phase, it invested heavily in product development and allowed marketing and service to fall down on the priority list. As the company shifted to a focus on Novation, finding different ways to connect with this partner was critical. For example, Neoforma invested resources to learn about the requirements and agreements created between Novation and its hospitals. Engineers and technicians also spent considerable effort learning about the back-end systems of the Novation hospitals.

During the brand phase, specific tactics are in place to identify "power users" (hospitals who use the technology on a daily basis) and to showcase their success with Neoforma products. The goal of these tactics is to demonstrate progress to both current and potential customers. Other tactics during this phase emphasize a focus on marketing to end users. Neoforma hired a vice president of marketing and is rebranding its products, including developing a new logo. Finally, service has become particularly important, as each end user has to feel supported by Neoforma.

Checking Our Progress. Organizations continually assess their effectiveness by measuring key indicators related to their drivers and their strategies. It is also important for organizations to attend to their future capability. Are there measures to indicate success (or not) in building that future capability?

In Neoforma, key performance measures have evolved along with the company. Certainly the development of the technology was the focus in the early days, and the critical measures revolved around product development. As the company shifted to a focus on

Novation, attention turned to measures related to the relationship with Novation (for example, the number of Novation hospitals that had adopted the technology). Finally, in this last phase, a critical measure is the number of power users.

These examples of Neoforma's movement through the strategy process are summarized in Tables 1.1, 1.2, and 1.3. Table 1.1 summarizes the elements of strategy as a learning process during Neoforma's technology phase.

Table 1.2 summarizes the same information during the partnership phase.

Table 1.3 provides a summary of the learning process elements during the brand phase.

Interestingly, although Neoforma executives describe themselves as going through these three critical phases, the knowledge of different phases was neither explicit nor intentional at the time,

**Table 1.1. Neoforma's Learning Process: Phase One—
Technology (1996–1999).**

Process Element	Example
Assessing Where We Are	Pressures in health care to reduce costs. Lack of even rudimentary IT tools in hospitals.
Understanding Who We Are and Where We Want to Go	A high-tech company with an Internet solution for the health care industry.
Learning How to Get There	Selling our technology to hospitals one at a time, business and leadership strategies built around developing and delivering the best technology.
Making the Journey	Significant investments in product development, power in the organization afforded to those in technology.
Checking Our Progress	Success in development of the technology.

**Table 1.2. Neoforma's Learning Process: Phase Two—
Partnership (2000–2002).**

Process Element	Example
Assessing Where We Are	Hesitancy in hospitals to invest in nonclinical applications.
	Hesitancy of suppliers to become involved unless guaranteed access to many hospitals.
	Existence of co-ops to offset costs and risks to hospitals and suppliers.
Understanding Who We Are and Where We Want to Go	A company that has partnered with a key organization to deliver our technology to the health care industry.
Learning How to Get There	Create a link to customers and suppliers and extend our reach in efficient ways by partnering with a key co-op (Novation).
Making the Journey	Tactics to immerse the mind-set, operations, and systems around Novation and its hospitals, such as learning about the back-end systems in these hospitals and creating a culture to support the Novation relationship (for example, using the language of the hospitals instead of the language of technology).
Checking Our Progress	Performance measures related to the relationship with Novation, number of Novation hospitals that had adopted the technology.

and the transitions from phase to phase were not perfect. Rather, in hindsight they can map the history of their organization to the cycle in Figure 1.2. It does not take having the knowledge of a process like that depicted in Figure 1.2 to create learning and focus in an organization, but having knowledge of this process allows a common language to exist within the organization and might make navigating that process a bit easier. Successfully driving this process—whether it is explicit or not—does require effective leadership, a type of leadership we call strategic leadership.

**Table 1.3. Neoforma's Learning Process: Phase Three—
Brand (2003 and Beyond).**

Process Element	Example
Assessing Where We Are	Conservative and skeptical nature of hospitals.
Understanding Who We Are and Where We Want to Go	A company that has succeeded in reducing costs in the health care industry, and one that can help other hospitals too.
Learning How to Get There	Extend reach to potential customers (to answer "proof" and "how") by driving the adoption of and reliance on our solutions in our installed base.
Making the Journey	Rebrand our products and services outside of Novation; develop key case studies of success with our installed base.
Checking Our Progress	Number of power users, growth in new offerings.

Implications for Strategic Leaders

Conceptualizing the strategy-making and implementation process as one of continuous learning is not new in the strategy literature. Henry Mintzberg has contributed significantly to our understanding of strategy making, and particularly to the idea that it includes a dimension of learning. He has helped clarify the distinction between *deliberate strategy*, which includes the more formalized and intentional elements of organizational strategy (for example, what you might find in a formal document, or explicitly articulated as official strategy) and *emergent strategy* (Mintzberg, 1987, 1998; Mintzberg & Waters, 1985). The latter involves strategy as it evolves in real-time practice, with or without conscious realization that what is being done in the interest of organizational success may not necessarily be consistent with expressed strategy. Others also have commented on how strategy-in-practice can change somewhat beyond individual or organizational awareness that it is happening: "Strategies develop over time through successive iterations of decisions and actions. Most of the time nobody even recognizes the strategic implications of what is going on until much later" (Floyd & Wooldridge, 1996, p. 38).

Despite the advice of Mintzberg, and despite the emphasis on organizational learning by Senge (1990) and others, we find in our work with executives that strategy is not often thought of as a learning process. In fact, when we ask executives to describe how strategy is crafted in their organizations, we get long descriptions of off-site retreats with agendas filled with rigorous steps and analyses. The outcome of such a retreat is often a strategic plan that is so long and involved it fills binders and weighs down shelves. Once the retreat is over, the binders tend to sit on the shelf and gather dust.

Why don't executives explicitly talk about strategy as a learning process? One reason may be that learning implies that something is not currently known—and the cultures of many organizations emphasize *knowing*. Aren't those who know the most those who are promoted? Other executives are open to learning yet feel there isn't time for it. The reality is that organizations must learn and those that have the best learning practices in place have a significant competitive advantage. As Peter Senge notes, "It is no longer sufficient to have one person learning for the organization, a Ford or a Sloan or a Watson. It's just not possible any longer to 'figure it out' from the top and have everyone else following the orders of the 'grand strategist.' The organizations that will excel in the future will be the organizations that discover how to tap people's commitment and capacity to learn at *all* levels in an organization" (1990, p. 4).

While there are many implications of viewing strategy as a learning process, we would like to explore four in particular:

- Leading strategy involves discovery more than determination.

- Strategic leadership is not reserved for those at the top.

- It's not enough to be a good strategic leader yourself; you have to foster strategic leadership in others, too.

- Strategic leaders blend the skills of thinking, acting, and influencing to drive strategy as a learning process in their organizations.

Discovery versus Determination

Several writers on strategy (for example, Beer & Eisenstat, 2000) talk about the process of defining strategy as if a person or group of people can go into a room, talk about what their strategy should be, and as long as it is clearly defined, all should be fine. The word *define* implies that we can sit back and determine what strategy is best for us. Many writers (for example, Treacy & Wiersema, 1995) have even gone so far as to define a limited number of categories of strategies (for example, product innovation, customer intimacy, and operational effectiveness) and declare that the work of leadership is to determine which one is right for the organization.

For most organizations, crafting strategy is more of a discovery process than it is a determination process or a process of choosing among a limited set of possibilities. It involves discovering the few key things the organization needs to do well and can do well to differentiate it in its industry.

In *Good to Great*, Jim Collins (2001) describes this process as coming to understand the "hedgehog principle," a term based on the Isaiah Berlin essay "The Hedgehog and the Fox." Berlin divided the world into foxes, who "know many things" and see the complexity of situations and create different strategies to deal with that complexity, and hedgehogs, who "know one big thing" and simplify the complexity of the world into one unifying concept. As Collins found, both good and great companies had strategies. However, while the good companies set theirs from bravado, the great companies set theirs from understanding. He summed up his findings with this statement: "A Hedgehog Concept is not a goal to be the best, a strategy to be the best, an intention to be the best, a plan to be the best. It is an *understanding* of what you *can* be the best at. The distinction is absolutely crucial" (p. 98).

Discovery takes discipline. Think again about your mental experiment with surfing. While you may feel exuberance about trying to conquer the waves and may be tempted to jump right in, you know that an expert surfer spends time watching the waves before ever attempting to catch one. It's necessary to learn about where the waves break. You work to understand the impact of the direction, speed, and fetch of the wind (the distance the wind blows over open water) on the size and shape of the waves. You get a sense of the waves' rhythm and the patterns underlying their progression. And this knowledge makes you even more energized about the possibilities; that is, you can actually fuel your exuberance with this disciplined learning.

Discipline is even more necessary in strategy and in business. Collins notes that coming to an understanding of the Hedgehog Concept is an iterative process that takes *four years* on average (2001, p. 114). Bravado, on the other hand, can happen instantaneously. Perhaps that is why it is so appealing.

This discovery process is modeled week after week in our DSL program. We use a business simulation where executives run a company called Hawley-Garcia. In the simulation, participants have use of a computer model to simulate five years of operations at the company. Over the course of those years, their articulation of the drivers and strategy of Hawley-Garcia changes as they come to a deeper understanding of the industry dynamics and their company's position in that industry. For example, early on one regional group articulated key points of its strategy as follows: "Maintain market share in the home market. Leverage alliances to become a leader in specialty tools." As their understanding deepened, they changed those key points: "Increase capacity and quality of manufacturing lines to support growth in high-end product lines while investing in research and development to support innovation." Those two statements are quite different. The first was essentially set through bravado—putting a stake in the ground with little understanding. The second evolved as they studied their industry, the key drivers in their region, and their region's role in the company overall. It represents a much more informed strategy.

Broad Reach

One of the myths of strategic leadership is that strategy is the CEO's job and others play little to no role in the process. Associated with this myth is the belief that the CEO and possibly the top leadership team go off for several days and come back with the strategy. True, the CEO is ultimately responsible for deciding upon a path for the organization. True, the CEO often involves some team of senior management in that decision-making process. But that does not mean that these people are the only strategic leaders within an organization. On the contrary, the CEO relies upon input and insights throughout the organization to set the strategy, to enact the strategy, and to help in understanding how well the strategy is working. The danger of this myth—that strategic leadership is reserved for those at the top—is that those lower in the organization will consciously or unconsciously believe it, will not see themselves as strategic leaders, and therefore will not behave as strategic leaders.

The plethora of big-name CEOs who have been very successful leading their companies—both past and present—perpetuates this myth. Names such as Henry Ford, Jack Welch, Lou Gerstner, and Andrew Carnegie bring to mind the image of people so bright and so good that they can single-handedly know the best direction for their companies, set the processes in motion to get there, and ensure that the company stays on track. However, more likely than not, these people were so good at leading their companies precisely because they relied on others.

Consider the case of Dennie Welsh. Does his name sound familiar? Probably not. In 1993, Dennie was running the Integrated Systems Services Corporation of IBM, that is, the services and network operations in the United States. While the fact that he was running a unit within IBM may sound big, his role was relatively small given the size and structure of IBM at the time. As Lou Gerstner indicates in *Who Says Elephants Can't Dance?*, "[This part of the organization was] a promising but minor part of IBM's portfolio. In fact, it wasn't even a stand-alone business in IBM. It was a sub-unit of the sales force" (2002, p. 129). So Dennie was not exactly a top manager within IBM.

Yet in many ways, Dennie can be credited with the major shift in IBM's strategy from a product company to a service company. Here is an excerpt from Gerstner's book, in which he describes a meeting with Dennie:

> It was our first private meeting, but he didn't waste much time on small talk. He told me that his vision of a services company was not one that did just IBM product maintenance and strung together computer codes for customers. He envisioned a company that would literally take over and act on behalf of the customers in all aspects of information technology—from building systems to defining architectures to actually managing the computers and running them for the customers.
>
> My mind was afire. Not only was he describing something I'd wanted when I was a customer (for example, I had tried unsuccessfully to outsource the running of RJR Nabisco's data centers), but this idea meshed exactly with our strategy of integration. Here was a man who understood what customers were willing to spend money on, and he knew what that meant—not just the business potential for IBM, but the coming restructuring of the industry around solutions rather than piece parts [pp. 129–130].

Gerstner might well have come upon this idea himself, given his desire to integrate the various parts of the company rather than sell them off; however, he did not need to do it himself. He had good people below him he could rely upon. And he recognized the need to rely upon those people.

When we think of how organizations have evolved over the past several decades, one of the key differences is that the lines between classic distinctions have become blurred—and rightly so. Trends such as concurrent engineering have emphasized the need for functions to work together, as opposed to the old model of having Marketing develop product specifications and then "throw them over the wall" to Engineering, who would develop the design and then "throw it over the wall" to Manufacturing for production. A better understanding of the needs and perspectives of the various functions allows the product to come to market more quickly and to meet customer needs more effectively—two outcomes that are critical for competitive advantage.

This blurring trend has happened with strategy making and strategy implementation too. That is, the line between *planner* and *implementer* has become blurred. The competitive forces in today's environment require us to be as in tune with our environment as possible, and often those who are at middle and lower levels of the organization are best suited to know the customer, competitors, and industry trends.

So strategy is not just the CEO's job. That is, strategic leadership is best exerted when information from the top is combined with information from the bottom ranks of the organization, and middle managers are in a unique position to do this. It is no wonder that more and more people throughout organizations are feeling the need to become more strategic.

Fostering Strategic Leadership

Just as it's a fallacy to believe that strategy is the job of just the CEO, it's wrong to believe that in order to enhance your own strategic leadership abilities you have to concentrate on building your own strategic skills. Being a strong strategic leader means you have to focus on others as much as—if not more than—on yourself.

Why this focus on others? Simple. The process of creating and sustaining competitive advantage in an organization is just too complex for any one person to develop and carry out. There is too much information to digest, the decisions are too complex, and success is too dependent on the blending of capabilities across the enterprise. This list could go on and on, but these two items go far enough in suggesting ways in which the strategic leader can focus on others:

- Create a climate that fosters strategic leadership in others.
- Develop strategic leadership abilities in those around you.

Many factors go into managing that first point, but one common example serves to illustrate: What is the climate in your organization for sharing information? Does information flow freely, so that people share their most honest opinions with each other, allowing those opinions to be shaped by data and perspectives of others? Beer and Eisenstat (2000) have researched what they call "silent killers" of strategy implementation and learning. Several of those silent killers are related to keeping things quiet in an organization—for example, a top-down management style and poor vertical communication. They cite Apple Computer as a prime example. It was known for several years in the 1980s that Microsoft was developing the Windows platform, which would compete with the Macintosh by providing less expensive access to similar technology. While managers throughout Apple were arguing for the need to develop and produce a low-end product, Beer and Eisenstat note their senior managers responded by yelling that this was wrong. This kind of response from any manager is virtually certain to inhibit information sharing.

With respect to developing strategic leadership abilities in those around you, we ask that you read this book with others in mind, perhaps at least one other person you are working with who needs to be more strategic. Think about ways you can apply the assessments and exercises throughout this book to guide this person's development. You might even consider working alongside that person as you both develop so that you can provide support to each other.

Driving Strategy as a Learning Process

The next three chapters will focus on how strategic leaders blend the skills of thinking, acting, and influencing to drive strategy as a learning process in their organizations. They use these skills throughout the cycle of learning to bring clarity and focus to the strategy, to enact that strategy with purpose and direction, and to engender the commitment of others to the future of the organization.

We have purposefully decided to devote a chapter each to thinking, acting, and influencing. This allows us to discuss specific competencies and perspectives related to each of these skills, and each skill's place in driving strategy as a learning process.

But it's important to clarify that thinking, acting, and influencing should not be viewed as separate and individual. It's not the case that a strategic leader first thinks to determine what to do, then acts to make the necessary decisions and choices associated with that thinking, and then influences others to get them on board. In reality, thinking, acting, and influencing are interdependent. That is, a strategic leader will take action that then informs future thinking about the strategy. (Indeed, this type of learning is the foundation of strategy as a learning process.) A strategic leader will also invite others into the strategy-making process—not just to facilitate their buy-in to the process but also to produce a better strategy than could have been developed in isolation. As you read the next three chapters, keep in mind the various ways that thinking, acting, and influencing work together. Each chapter will conclude with a discussion of that interdependency to help you make that connection.

Chapter Two

Strategic Thinking

What do Bill Gates of Microsoft and Peter Jackson, producer and director of *The Lord of the Rings* movie trilogy, have in common? Surely one characteristic common to both of them is vision. From an early age Bill Gates had a vision of the future of personal computing, and that vision helped shape an industry. When Peter Jackson read *The Lord of the Rings* trilogy at the age of eighteen, he couldn't wait until the books were made into movies. Twenty years later he made them himself.

Another characteristic these two creative leaders share is the ability to take stock of their present positions and anticipate what lies beyond the horizon—to scan their environment. They are also gifted at questioning implicit beliefs and assumptions. Both have to deal with the complexity that's part of a visionary enterprise, and both are skilled at making common sense for their organizations and teams, and at thinking systemically to uncover the answers to complex problems.

When we ask executives to mention a quality of great strategic leaders, the most common answer we hear is "vision." Another common answer is "good long-range planning." Both these attributes involve thinking skills, but they represent rather different kinds of thinking skills.

Long-range planning exemplifies the kind of strategic thinking that has been common in organizations for a long time, even if long-range planning itself has recently become somewhat less common. It tends to be analytical, linear, verbal (or numeric), explicit, and emotionally neutral. It is also relatively well developed among business leaders today. Vision, however, represents a different and less developed form of strategic thinking.

In the first part of this chapter we'll focus on the nature of this neglected kind of strategic thinking. Later we will turn our attention to how you can develop this type of strategic thinking. We will examine five strategic thinking competencies that will enhance your effectiveness as a strategic leader. These competencies represent some of the more creative aspects of a strategic leader's cognitive toolkit.

The Artful Nature of Strategic Thinking

Strategic thinking refers to cognitive processes required for the collection, interpretation, generation, and evaluation of information and ideas that shape an organization's sustainable competitive advantage. It's one of the three processes driving strategic learning in organizations (along with strategic acting and influencing), which means that strategic thinking involves a collective dimension as well as an individual one. In other words, for organizations to develop sustainable competitive advantage, it's not enough to have great individual strategic thinkers. It also takes individuals who influence one another's thinking, deepening and enhancing their collective understanding and insight. That's because the complex and changing nature of the competitive environment increasingly requires bringing diverse perspectives to bear on business challenges.

Unfortunately, the cognitive tools that strategic leaders have relied upon to accomplish these tasks have been unnecessarily constrained. A whole class of tools has been left out of their toolkits, and it's virtually impossible to make strategy a learning process in an organization without them.

Think of it this way: There is a "soft side" as well as a "hard side" to strategic leadership and strategic thinking. In general, the hard side of strategic thinking involves the kind of rigorous analytical tools and techniques taught in business schools. But strategic thinking has a softer side that is also a vital part of understanding and developing strategy, vision and values, culture and climate. The word *softer* does not imply weakness but rather includes those qualitative thinking skills that are held in opposition to hard-minded, quantitative rigor.

It's partly what Carly Fiorina, the CEO of Hewlett-Packard, had in mind when she told MIT's graduating class in 2000, "At any one moment in time you often can't see where your path is heading and logic and intellect alone won't lead you to make the right choices, won't in fact take you down the right path. You have to master not only the art of listening to your head, you must also master listening to your heart and listening to your gut."

Fiorina was speaking to graduates embarking on their lives as well as embarking on work, and her advice reflected wisdom of the unforeseeable twists and turns life takes. But her words also reflect today's business reality. Planning and implementing strategic change is becoming harder than ever, given the increasing pace of change, the increasing uncertainty about the future, and the increasing complexity of challenges faced by organizations in both the corporate and nonprofit sectors. Virtually every organization today faces complex challenges that defy existing solutions, mental models, resources, and approaches. Leaders today must learn to apply their full range of strategic thinking competencies to the complex challenges their organizations are facing, and to supplement analytical skills with a multifaceted understanding that includes the following insights:

- Strategic thinking requires synthesis as well as analysis.
- Strategic thinking is nonlinear as well as linear.
- Strategic thinking is visual as well as verbal.
- Strategic thinking is implicit as well as explicit.
- Strategic thinking engages the heart as well as the head.

Synthesis and Analysis

Analysis involves the breaking down of something into its constituent elements. It's a very useful skill, and one at which most managers are quite proficient. Synthesis, on the other hand, refers to the combination of separate elements into a more complex whole. Many managers today are considerably less practiced and competent in synthesis than in analysis. But creating strategy depends on synthesis as much as on analysis.

Perhaps an analogy here might help. A concert can be broken down into the separate parts played by each individual instrument. And not only can it be, but it needs to be in order for the musicians to practice their separate parts effectively. But that's not enough. The concert itself—at least a good one—depends upon skilled craftsmanship combining the separate elements into a pleasing and coherent whole. In a good concert the whole is more than the sum of its parts, and the same is true for strategy.

Strategy reflects choices between what an organization will do (or will be) and won't do (or won't be). Only certain patterns of choices, or combinations of alternative investments, contribute to a coherent whole (a viable strategy). For example, the pattern of choices a company might invest in to enact a strategy of product innovation would be quite different from the pattern of choices it would invest in to be the low-cost producer in the industry. Among other places, strategic synthesis occurs in the *learning how to get there* phase of strategy as a learning process.

Nonlinear and Linear

Linear thinking involves looking for (or assuming) cause-and-effect or sequential relationships between things, as in the form "A follows B." This is a valid and useful approach to many strategic problems. For example, projecting future sales by incremental adjustments to past sales often works quite effectively—but not always. What if your competitor launches a new product that makes yours woefully unattractive to customers? Such events represent discontinuities for which linear thinking—basing future plans and actions on past experience—is inappropriate. Linear thinking cannot solve challenges in a nonlinear world.

One dramatic example is our altered understanding of the threat of terrorism after 9/11. Prior to that day, terrorism seemed a relatively distant threat to most U.S. citizens. It occurred elsewhere in the world—in "trouble spots." Afterward, however, the greatest threat to the United States was no longer posed by one or two militarily powerful enemy nation-states. Rather, we perceived that we had become vulnerable to a coalition of loosely coordinated yet highly adaptable terrorist cells operating somewhat clandestinely throughout the world (Sanders, 2002).

The world of business, too, is increasingly defined by surprise and uncertainty. Most organizations have grown accustomed to the idea of fairly continuous change, and now the challenge is to learn to deal not only with continuous change but with *disruptive change*: events such as the 9/11 terrorist attacks, the SARS outbreak, and the Northeast power grid failure. "It is no longer just the pace of change but the disruptiveness of that change that demands our attention. . . . Rapid change can at least be anticipated, such as improvements in computing speed or capacity, but severe shocks and surprises such as that of '9/11' can destabilize entire industries and economies in a matter of hours or days" (McCann, 2004, p. 46). Succeeding in such environments requires nonlinear as well as linear thinking.

Visual and Verbal

As noted earlier, many people associate the word *vision* with strategic leadership. Less frequently do people fully appreciate the essential meaning of the word itself: having a vision is about *seeing* something. The greatest visionaries are those who are able to paint a picture of a more desirable future. Vivid words and phrases rich in imagery help them convey that picture.

The power of visual images in business is evident in effective brand images like the lonely Maytag repairman or the Verizon worker trekking through the wilderness asking, "Can you hear me now?" Visual thinking is also a useful way to explore strategic ideas. Two of our colleagues at CCL, Chuck Palus and David Horth, have developed a simple and powerful tool for tapping this visual dimension of thought in rich and constructive ways (see a full account of their work in Palus & Horth, 2002). The tool is called *Visual Explorer*, a set of several hundred diverse photographs and art reproductions selected for their visual richness and potential metaphorical association with varied business and personal challenges.

We frequently use *Visual Explorer* to facilitate conversations among executives about different business issues. We might begin, for example, by asking each of them to think about a strategic challenge facing his or her organization and then to select a picture that depicts in some way an aspect of that challenge. Almost always those conversations take on a richness and depth that is missing in the primarily verbal and often abstract conversations typical in most business meetings. For example, one participant who was responsible for transforming his organization's IT function selected a picture of bumper-to-bumper traffic on a congested highway. The group's discussion brought up issues like the relative disconnectedness among passengers in all the cars, confusion about where they've been and where they're going, suspicions about whether they like the trip they're taking—all relevant to the business issues this leader was facing.

Implicit and Explicit

We all know more than we are able to put into words. Whether they call it intuition, instinct, or "trusting your gut," effective leaders have learned to trust their judgment even when they are not able to make their rationale explicit. This ability becomes particularly important as leaders move into roles and positions of strategic responsibility in their organizations.

CCL has collected and analyzed data on the thinking styles of thousands of executives who have attended our programs, and it is interesting to examine how they vary in personal preference for dealing with information in relatively more explicit or implicit ways. Some prefer to make decisions in the context of well-defined problems using information that is objective, factual, concrete, and unambiguous. They especially trust their practicality and past experience. Others prefer to make decisions in the context of ill-defined problems by focusing more on patterns and relationships in data rather than on specific pieces of data. They especially trust their insight and imagination.

Our data indicate a somewhat greater representation at top levels of management of individuals whose natural preference is toward trusting their insight and imagination. Slightly over half of middle and upper-middle managers have this preference, and 60 percent at the senior executive level do. By comparison, more than two-thirds of the general population prefer to rely on their sense of practicality and past experience.

These differences are consistent with our understanding of the nature of strategic thinking. The strategic challenges that executives confront are often novel, complex, and ambiguous. For that reason, strategic decisions are often not entirely data driven; they demand executive judgment that attends to the best information available but rarely can be determined solely by it. In other words, strategic thinking is implicit as well as explicit.

Heart and Head

There is an old story about two stonemasons working side by side, each putting bricks together with mortar. Asked what they were doing, one said, "I'm laying bricks." The other said, "I'm building a cathedral." Don't you think that those answers reflect different degrees to which those workers were engaged in their work? When an activity has personal significance, we throw ourselves into it more completely than when it's "just a job."

The extent to which people throw themselves into work is a function of many things, but partly depends on whether the organization has clear and compelling aspirations. Articulating organizational aspirations that inspire members to higher levels and quality of effort is one of the key tasks of strategic leadership.

Organizational aspirations involve *understanding who we are and where we want to go*. We have emphasized the value of developing and communicating a vision that people can see, and one big reason it's important is that a vivid vision can touch hearts as well as heads. An organization's aspirations can give meaning to the work and energize people to do more than they thought they could or would.

That's why vision or mission statements that are merely quantitative in nature so frequently leave people uninspired (to be number one in the industry, for example, or to improve earnings). Imagine that you work for a pharmaceutical company. A goal might be to double sales—not a bad goal in itself. But quantitative goals like that rarely engage the whole person. Compare it with the examples in Exhibit 2.1—aspirational statements that touch the heart as well as the head.

Exhibit 2.1. Examples of Organizational Aspirations.

Xerox: Helping people find better ways to do great work.

Celestial Seasonings: To create and sell healthful, naturally oriented products that nurture people's bodies and uplift their souls.

Bristol-Myers Squibb: To extend and enhance human life.

Starbucks: To become the most recognizable brand in the world.

A church choir: To be a choir with a transformational impact on listener and member alike.

Summing Up

One of the challenges to developing your strategic thinking is that historically organizations have tended not to encourage and reinforce the two complementary sides of strategic thinking with anything like equality. Thus you might not have had much opportunity to practice or observe certain kinds of strategic thinking at work. You can get an idea about that by just scanning the two groups of words in Exhibit 2.2 to see whether one set captures the typical kind of strategic thinking in your organization more than the other.

Exhibit 2.2. Words for Thought Processes.	
Traditional Strategic Thinking Words	Complementary Mode Strategic Thinking Words
Observe	Reflect
Compare	Connect
Test	Create
Data	Pattern
Discuss	Visualize
Plan	Illustrate
Identify	Brainstorm
Assess	Represent
Define	Imagine
Outline	Demonstrate
Analyze	Synthesize
Classify	Associate
Manage	Integrate
Evaluate	Simulate

If you're like most managers, the set on the left is more characteristic of the kinds of thinking words people in your organization are accustomed to using. Nonetheless, both kinds of thinking competencies are required of strategic leaders today. The rest of this chapter is about developing these less developed competencies. Before you begin the next section, we suggest you assess your strategic thinking skills with the brief survey in Exhibit 2.3.

Exhibit 2.3. Evaluate Your Strategic Thinking Skills.

For each of these behaviors, use the following scale to assess your need to improve in that area.

1	2	3	4	5
Considerable Improvement Needed		Moderate Improvement Needed		No Improvement Needed

Scan the environment for forces and trends that could impact the organization's competitiveness.

        1   2   3   4   5

Ensure that all necessary information is considered.

        1   2   3   4   5

See things in new and different ways.

        1   2   3   4   5

Identify the truly key facts or trends amid the large amount of data available to be considered.

        1   2   3   4   5

Understand your own biases and do not let them play too strong of a role in your thinking.

        1   2   3   4   5

Identify key points or issues and discern the truly significant information among the explosion of data confronting you.

        1   2   3   4   5

See patterns and relationships between seemingly disparate data, and ask probing questions about the interactive effects among various parts of the business.

        1   2   3   4   5

Offer original, creative ideas.

        1   2   3   4   5

Developing Your Strategic Thinking

Thus far we have been exploring the two sides of strategic thinking, with particular attention to its less familiar, artful elements. Now we turn our attention to your developing competencies to help build and apply that less familiar side.

When we work with managers and executives, we usually ask them to describe their own greatest challenges to becoming a better strategic leader. Here are a few representative responses:

- To develop a vision for where my organization needs to be in five years
- To have a broader perspective on the competitive landscape
- To step back and see the big picture
- To be more comfortable thinking out of the box

We also pay attention during our work to what aspects of strategy as a learning process are most challenging and most helpful for managers and executives to understand and learn to apply. Based on this experience, we have identified five strategic thinking competencies that we believe are integrally embedded in the broader challenge of strategic leadership and typically least developed:

- Scanning
- Visioning
- Reframing
- Making common sense
- Systems thinking

Collectively, these strategic thinking competencies also tap the aspects of strategic thinking that we've noted are vital yet underdeveloped in most managers (Linkow, 1999). Scanning and systems thinking both involve nonlinear thinking. Visioning strives to touch the heart as well as the head. Reframing often depends upon implicit thinking, and also can involve visual thinking. And making common sense requires synthesis more than analysis. Now we will look more closely at the nature of each of these five strategic thinking competencies as well as at how to develop them.

Scanning

Though the strategic learning process can actually begin anywhere, it typically begins with assessing where the organization is. This involves examining the organization's current strategic situation, and it includes an analysis of the opportunities and threats in the industry as well as the strengths and weaknesses inside the organization. This is commonly called a SWOT analysis; the acronym stands for strengths, weaknesses, opportunities, and threats. A more detailed description of a SWOT analysis is presented in Exhibit 2.4.

Exhibit 2.4. SWOT Analysis.

SWOT analysis is a common method for *assessing where we are* (see Figure 2.1 on page 57). Here's a closer look at the SWOT analysis elements:

Strengths. What internal capabilities or assets give the organization a competitive advantage? In what ways does the organization serve its key internal and external stakeholders well?

Weaknesses. What internal capabilities or assets is the organization relatively ineffective or inefficient at performing or possessing, or so limited in capacity as to put it at a competitive disadvantage? In what ways does the organization fall short in serving key internal and external stakeholders?

Opportunities. What conditions or possible future conditions in the external environment might give the organization a competitive advantage and enhance achievement of its vision if taken advantage of?

Threats. What conditions or possible future conditions in the external environment might put the organization at a competitive disadvantage and inhibit achievement of its vision if steps are not taken to minimize their impact?

To see how this works, go through an exercise like the one described in Exhibit 2.5.

This organizational examination and analysis is sometimes called *environmental scanning*. It's not unlike what sailors did in the age of wooden ships—having a man in the crow's nest with a telescope to scan the horizon for sight of land or another ship, a ship that could be friend or foe. It's a vital organizational competency to master, lest the organization fail to recognize and take advantage of strategic opportunities or, on the other hand, fail to recognize and thus fall prey to strategic threats.

For the individual manager, scanning as a strategic thinking competency involves attending to the informational horizon beyond one's own job, team, division, function, company, or even industry. Unlike an organizational SWOT analysis, which tends to be relatively systematic, individual scanning is apt to be quite

---

Exhibit 2.5. SWOT Conversations.

Do a SWOT analysis on your own organization (examine your organization's internal strengths and weaknesses, and the opportunities and threats facing you in the external environment). Then have conversations with four other individuals from your organization:

- Someone two levels senior to you
- Someone from a different functional area
- Someone with a reputation for creative or "out of the box" business thinking
- A manager with a reputation for being solid and levelheaded

Ask each of them independently what they consider your company's three or four most strategically important strengths, weaknesses, opportunities, and threats, and also what overall strategic implications they draw from their respective analyses. Compare their responses with each other as well as with your own analysis. What were the points of agreement? What were the points of disagreement? What did you learn about your own insight and appreciation for your organization's strategic situation?

nonlinear. The point is to be looking all around, to be vigilant for potentially useful information anywhere.

Good strategic thinkers scan their environments for data, trends, or ideas that could potentially have significance for their organization's future competitiveness.

To put it differently, scanning involves freeing yourself from the silos you may have erected in your mind and looking beyond self-imposed constraints that focus attention on information within a limited domain. Good strategic thinkers often scan diverse sources of information, such as magazines and journals outside their business or industry literature. They seek out perspectives from others involved in diverse kinds of work. They can sift through information quickly, not necessarily deeply but with an eye for the anomalous or otherwise interesting bit of data.

Scanning is especially useful in both the elements of strategy as a learning process highlighted in Figure 2.1. As noted, a SWOT analysis is a common approach to *assessing where we are*. Furthermore, emergent strategy typically arises based on discoveries or adaptations made when *making the journey*, so scanning is useful there too.

Visioning

A vision represents a view of what the organization (or a department, group, or other unit) can and should become. There can be formal expressions of organizational aspiration, as in official vision statements or core values. At the same time, however, many individuals also hold personal but unspoken versions of organizational aspirations. Unfortunately, they seldom share these personal visions. Knowing the different implicit aspirations individuals have for their organization can be informative and even inspiring. As an example, consider our work with the leadership team at Harlequin, a publisher of women's fiction (most notably in the romance genre) and subsidiary of the Canadian communications company Torstar. During an off-site strategic planning session we asked each of the

Figure 2.1. Strategy as a Learning Process: Where We Are.

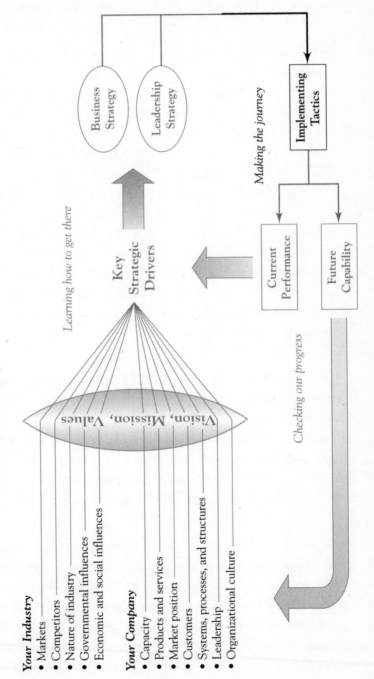

Assessing where we are

Understanding who we are and where we want to go

Your Industry
• Markets
• Competitors
• Nature of industry
• Governmental influences
• Economic and social influences

Your Company
• Capacity
• Products and services
• Market position
• Customers
• Systems, processes, and structures
• Leadership
• Organizational culture

Vision, Mission, Values

Key Strategic Drivers

Learning how to get there

Business Strategy

Leadership Strategy

Making the journey

Implementing Tactics

Current Performance

Future Capability

Checking our progress

dozen executives on the team to compose his or her own individual version of Harlequin's future. Our specific instructions:

> Your assignment is to write a one-page newspaper article portraying your vision and aspirations for Harlequin. The article should represent what would make you proud to be able to say or write about Harlequin three or four years from now. Therefore, each of you should write your own version of that article (that might be published in, for example, the *Toronto Star* or *The Wall Street Journal* in 2007), describing Harlequin's achievements.
>
> Write this article so that it tells the story of Harlequin's success and is not merely a list of "bullet points" or specific facts and achievements. Write the story so that it evokes feelings of pride when you read it, and conveys a sense of what kind of company Harlequin is, as well as what it has accomplished. As any good journalist would, of course, you will want to cite a variety of supporting material including quotes, business results, anecdotes about corporate culture and morale, etc.

As we expected, the team initially balked a bit at these instructions and lobbied to merely outline their respective organizational visions with a few bullet points. They acceded to our approach, however, and were amazed and pleased at the quality and richness of input, across the board. Here is an excerpt from one of their articles, set in the personalized form of a communiqué about Harlequin from Oprah Winfrey on her Web site:

> When I walked into the Harlequin office in Toronto, I came face-to-face with a floor-to-ceiling sign that read World Domination of Women's Fiction. And I thought *I* had big goals! But as I walked around the office, I felt not a sense of domination, but of appreciation. Appreciation for the passion of reading, for all the people that bring passion to life for millions of readers, and for the skill and talent that it takes to accomplish that. All the while Harlequin is

demonstrating this appreciation, it continues to sell more books every year—over 200 million at last count. On Friday I'll share with you some of my encounters with the people who help Harlequin put the entertainment back into reading.

Harlequin is my kind of company—one that cares about its family of readers, and its employees, and can still be successful. And on top of that, it provides me all of the entertaining fiction I could ever dream of wanting. I can't believe it took me this long to discover Harlequin—and now I can't imagine my world without it. Take a moment to introduce yourself to a new friend—you'll have this one for life.

O.

It's sometimes said that vision must come from the top. Perhaps, but it's also true that activities like those described in Exhibit 2.6 can enrich the vision-setting process. It affords broader opportunity for people to share personal versions of aspirations for the organization. It also can inform people throughout the organization

---

**Exhibit 2.6. Suggestions for Development:
Craft Your Own Organization's Story.**

Compare your own aspirations for your organization with others using the newspaper article technique described in this chapter. Have a group at work craft their own individual versions of your organization's story following instructions similar to those used in the Harlequin illustration. After the stories are completed, share and discuss them and use them as a springboard for developing a shared vision.

Individuals in the group can exchange their respective articles and note points of correspondence as well as differences. They can use questions to guide their reading, such as these: How high are your aspirations for the organization? What are the biggest differences between the current organizational reality and your (and others') aspirations? Were there ways that others saw the organization changing that did not occur to you? What could make you more conscious of changes like those whether or not you see them as desirable?

of the many different possibilities and visions that can exist simultaneously (not necessarily inconsistently) within one organization. Perhaps most important, an activity like this can generate collective inspiration for an organization's future, even amid differing individual versions of it.

Since visioning is so closely connected to organizational aspirations, it's especially useful in *understanding who we are and where we want to go*, as depicted in Figure 2.2.

Reframing

Reframing involves the ability to see things differently, including new ways of thinking about an organization's strategic challenges and basic capabilities. It involves questioning or restating the implicit beliefs and assumptions that are often taken for granted by organization members. It plays a critical role in the *formative* phases of the strategic learning process from *assessing where we are* through *learning how to get there*, as highlighted in Figure 2.3. The process often uses metaphors like those outlined in Exhibit 2.7.

Reframing the Nature of the Business at Yellow Freight.   One example of strategic reframing involves Yellow Freight, a trucking company that transports big, heavy freight. In 1995, Yellow Freight suffered its worst year in the company's history. A new CEO helped turn the company around, and a key part of the effort involved learning that its assumptions about its customers were all wrong (Salter, 2002).

Previously, the company had "known" that price and speed of delivery were what mattered most to its customers. When it eventually surveyed a large sample of customers, however, the company learned that reliability and quality were what mattered most: for pickup and delivery to be reliable and for goods to arrive undamaged. Yellow Freight's trouble had boiled down in large part to what Will Rogers called "knowing what ain't so." Its new CEO reframed how Yellow Freight thought about itself: it used to think of itself as

Figure 2.2. Strategy as a Learning Process: Who We Are.

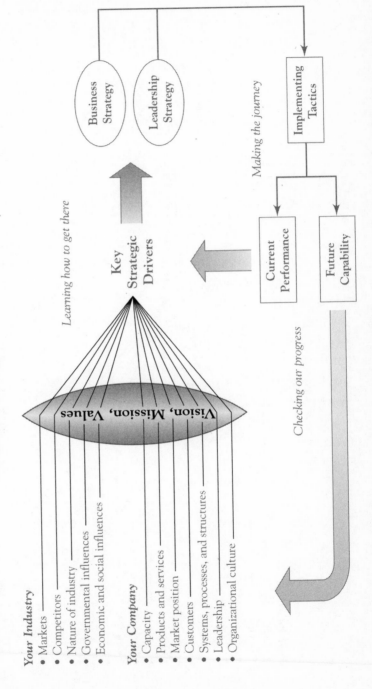

Understanding who we are and where we want to go

Assessing where we are

Your Industry
- Markets
- Competitors
- Nature of industry
- Governmental influences
- Economic and social influences

Your Company
- Capacity
- Products and services
- Market position
- Customers
- Systems, processes, and structures
- Leadership
- Organizational culture

Vision, Mission, Values

Key Strategic Drivers

Learning how to get there

Business Strategy

Leadership Strategy

Implementing Tactics

Making the journey

Current Performance

Future Capability

Checking our progress

Figure 2.3. Strategy as a Learning Process: How to Get There.

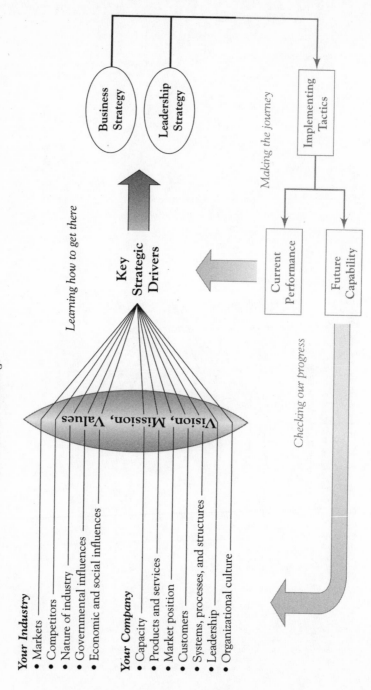

Assessing where we are

Understanding who we are and where we want to go

Your Industry
• Markets
• Competitors
• Nature of industry
• Governmental influences
• Economic and social influences

Your Company
• Capacity
• Products and services
• Market position
• Customers
• Systems, processes, and structures
• Leadership
• Organizational culture

Vision, Mission, Values

Learning how to get there

Key Strategic Drivers

Business Strategy

Leadership Strategy

Implementing Tactics

Making the journey

Current Performance

Future Capability

Checking our progress

Exhibit 2.7. Suggestion for Development: Using Metaphors.

Complex phenomena like leadership are often grasped more easily through the use of metaphor. Many different kinds of metaphors are used to describe leadership. Here are a few:

- Leadership as combat
- Leadership as sport
- Leadership as art
- Leadership as a machine
- Leadership as gardening

Use metaphors to describe strategic leadership in your organization. Explore how one—or several—of these metaphors might describe some aspect of your organization's approach to leadership.

---

a company in the trucking business, but now it thinks of itself as a company in the service business that uses trucks.

Reframing the Nature of the Business at Starbucks. Reframing can be an essential part of resolving an organizational dilemma, but it also can be experienced as unhelpful and disruptive to those who may not perceive any dilemma.

Starbucks began in 1971 as a very different company from the one we know today. The difference is due in large part to the way its chairman, Howard Schultz, reframed the kind of business Starbucks should be in. Schultz joined Starbucks in 1982 to head its marketing and retail store operations. While on a trip to Italy in 1983, Schultz was amazed by the number and variety of espresso bars there—fifteen hundred in the city of Turin alone. He concluded that the Starbucks stores in Seattle had missed the point; *Starbucks should not be just a store but an experience—a gathering place.*

Everything looks clearer in hindsight, of course, but the Starbucks owners resisted Schultz's vision; Starbucks was a retailer, they insisted, not a restaurant or bar. His strategic reframing of the Starbucks opportunity was ultimately vindicated when, having left

Starbucks to pursue the same idea with another company, Schultz had the opportunity to purchase the whole Starbucks operation in Seattle, including its name.

Exhibit 2.8 provides an exercise in strategic reframing.

Exhibit 2.8. Suggestion for Development: Strategic Reframing.

Prompt your own reframing of strategic leadership issues by asking yourself questions like these:

- What would we do differently if we *really* listened to our customers?
- What are some different ways we can think about what *quality* means in our work?
- What could we be the best in the world at doing? How might doing that change the nature of our organization?
- Instead of thinking about ourselves as an organization that [fill in how you currently characterize your work], what if we thought about ourselves as an organization that [fill in a different way of thinking about what your organization does].
- Have certain processes and activities in our organization merely become ends in themselves rather than means to an end?
- Ask yourself, "Is our structure serving our strategy, or is our strategy serving our structure?"
- Use the idea of the inverted pyramid organization as a metaphor (that is, instead of thinking of the senior leaders at the top of the pyramid and being "served by" everyone else in the organization, think about senior leaders as the bottom of the pyramid and serving everyone else). What else might it be helpful to "turn upside down"?

Reframing Decisions Advantageously. Research on decision making indicates that how decisions are framed makes a significant difference in the decisions made. Even the mere labeling of external conditions as opportunities or threats can change the ways people respond to them. For example, the perception of external conditions as opportunities tends to broaden organizational participation in the response and evoke decisions representing relatively small changes that are directed at the external environment. When conditions are perceived as threats, however, organizational response tends to occur in a top-down manner evoking much larger-scale responses, often involving more significant internal changes (Floyd & Wooldridge, 1996).

Research has shown that one of the most powerful factors affecting decisions is whether the stakes are framed as potential gains or potential losses. Daniel Kahneman and Amos Tversky developed a paradigm for decision research that has stimulated numerous studies of this dynamic. Here's the kind of problem used in this research (see Hammond, Keeney, & Raiffa, 1998):

Say, for example, that you are responsible for the installation of a new IT system in your organization at three separate operating locations. Unfortunately, you have discovered that a computer virus has infected the system. The virus seems resistant to all existing countermeasures, and the entire system will be lost if the virus is not successfully countered in the next twenty-four hours. The value of the system at each location is $1 million. A new virus detection company may be able to save all your equipment, but the result is not certain. The company gives you two options.

Option 1: This will save the equipment at one of the sites, worth $1 million. The equipment at the other two sites will be lost.

Option 2: This has a one-third chance of saving the computer equipment at all three locations, worth $3 million. But it has a two-thirds chance of losing the computers everywhere.

Given these alternatives, more than 70 percent of people choose the "less risky" first option. But what if the choices had been different? What would you do if instead you'd been given these choices?

Option 3: This will lose all of the computers at two of the locations, worth $2 million. The equipment at one of the two locations will be saved.

Option 4: This has a two-thirds chance of losing the computers at all three locations, worth $3 million, but a one-third chance of saving everything.

Faced with these choices, 80 percent of people choose option 4. That is intriguing, especially when you realize—as you probably did here—that the two pairs of alternatives are identical and merely framed in different ways. The different patterns of responses reflect a strong aversion to taking risk when a choice is framed in terms of gains (computers saved) but a willingness to take risk when avoiding losses (computers ruined). People tend to avoid risks when they are seeking gains, but they choose risks to avoid sure losses. This finding implies that you shouldn't automatically accept the way an issue is initially framed. Explore alternative ways of framing the problem to see whether that makes a difference in the relative attractiveness or apparent desirability of the options.

The Value of Reframing.   The value of reframing depends on the situation and context. In becoming a strategic leader, you must adapt your personal inclination to reframe an issue with the needs of the situation. (Is reframing actually required?)

People differ in terms of their preferences about how to approach change. Some prefer change that is fairly methodical and cautious, whereas others prefer change that is more expansive and immediate. Those who prefer methodical and cautious change also tend to be most comfortable working within a particular paradigm or framework, whereas those who prefer more expansive and immediate change tend to see things differently and want to reframe things. Greater awareness about your own preferred approach to change leads to insights about when and how your penchant for seeing things differently may be most helpful. In some lines of work, for example, constantly generating new ways of seeing things may be particularly unhelpful. We recall an operations manager at a nuclear reactor who said, "In our work there is a fine line between vision and hallucination."

As part of our DSL program we give participants feedback about their preferred approaches to change. We always highlight how different managers vary considerably in their preferences and underscore how all preferences make distinctly valuable contributions to the change process—it's not a matter of good preference or bad preference. Invariably, these insights about change preferences give leaders a new way of understanding the source of tension they've experienced with others when trying to agree upon or implement change. When people who prefer expansive and immediate change suggest a fairly dramatic reframing of a situation, it may create tension with those with a different change style. And when people who prefer more methodical and cautious change resist reframing, that can create tension with their counterparts too.

Making Common Sense

One of the most important things leaders do—especially strategic leaders—is to help others in their organizations make sense of the world around them, the challenges they collectively face, and how they will face them together. Increasingly, groups and organizations face problems and challenges that belie easy definition and resist routine solutions. When facing ambiguous situations or ill-defined problems, the temptation of many leaders might be to create structure and certainty by imposing a personal view of the situation: in a sense, to make everyone else adopt their own sense of it. In truly ambiguous situations, however, that's often a dangerous path to take. In the long run it is often more constructive to *make common sense* of the situation—meaning to create a shared understanding of the situation, not to assume one person's interpretation of it is correct.

In our work with executives we often use an outdoor activity called *orienteering*—finding a route across unfamiliar back country without an established trail—which gives them many opportunities to create shared meaning. For example, those unfamiliar with hiking in some of the terrain found in Colorado Springs at the foothills of the Rocky Mountains do not always discern the significance of contour lines on their topographical maps (when contour lines are close together, for example, it indicates steep terrain). Similarly, reaching consensus as to where they are as an orienteering team often involves all the members of the team sharing how they interpret different sorts of clues in their physical environment and then indicating where they believe that puts them on the map.

Strategic leadership requires making common sense amid complex and ambiguous conditions. The dynamic challenges facing organizations today contribute to a common experience of lack of clarity about direction and alignment, and a sense of disorganization and confusion. Strategic leadership involves making common sense amid just such chaotic conditions. It involves giving some coherence to what could otherwise feel like confusing and contradictory communications and signals at work. Like reframing, making common sense is particularly useful during the earlier stages of strategy as a learning process, as highlighted in Figure 2.4.

Developing shared understanding is important because people often rely on implicit knowledge rather than on explicit knowledge when it comes to communicating or sharing ideas. Unarticulated knowledge can cause people to feel unclear or confused about the apparent disconnectedness between the priorities, policies, and processes of different teams, departments, or divisions in their organization. This is less likely to happen when people share a common understanding of their vision and strategy.

At work, people need to make common sense about a whole range of things:

- Their vision of the future
- Their understanding of challenges facing the organization
- Guidance from higher authority
- How the team will interface with other individuals and groups
- Obstacles to group or team success, and ways to overcome them

Figure 2.4. Strategy as a Learning Process: Making Common Sense.

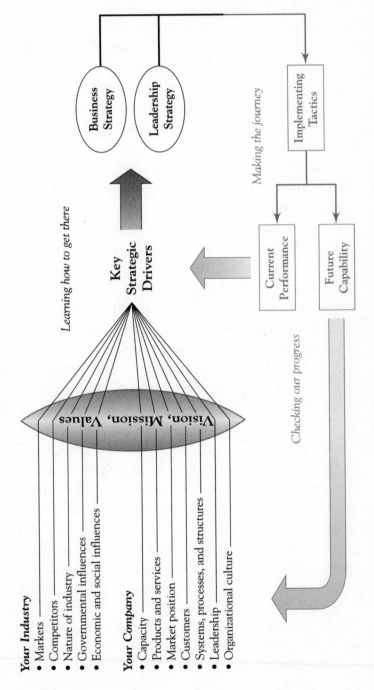

Assessing where we are

Understanding who we are and where we want to go

Your Industry
• Markets
• Competitors
• Nature of industry
• Governmental influences
• Economic and social influences

Your Company
• Capacity
• Products and services
• Market position
• Customers
• Systems, processes, and structures
• Leadership
• Organizational culture

Vision, Mission, Values

Key Strategic Drivers

Learning how to get there

Business Strategy

Leadership Strategy

Implementing Tactics

Making the journey

Current Performance

Future Capability

Checking our progress

Making Common Sense in a Hospital.   A large independent health care facility had an excellent reputation in its community but was trying to position itself favorably amid new competition, regulations, technologies, and a changing demographic characterized by immigration and aging. The hospital's senior management articulated a new vision of becoming a customer-focused hospital. The technical elements of such a vision were benchmarked, but the implications for social and cultural change at this conservative organization seemed daunting.

The senior team was thinking about a leadership strategy to support its new vision. Mindful of a need to broaden participation in this initiative, it invited a number of directors to a retreat. Some of those who attended were surprised by the format of the retreat. They had thought they would be briefed by the CEO on a management direction for the hospital and then given guidance about how the change would be managed. But the retreat, although deeply concerned with direction and leadership, was focused on sense making and on using dialogue as the means to achieve it.

The group started by looking at the results of an internal climate survey and hearing about the key challenges facing the hospital as viewed by the different people in the room. They listed sacred cows—the maddening quirks of work at the hospital that are typically not to be questioned in public. They asked: Why have we come together? What are we seeing? What's missing? Why change?

As the dialogue moved to more difficult topics, an improvised change in the room setup proved especially helpful. The group moved from behind the long tables into a circle of chairs. Body language became more obvious. Several members of the group said they felt more exposed. One person said, "Now it feels more like a meeting of hearts and minds and less like a standard business conversation."

The group then used the *Visual Explorer* activity (described earlier in this chapter). Each person examined dozens of pictures clipped from magazines and the Internet, which were spread out around the room so people could browse through them. The instruction was for each of them to pick a picture or two that somehow captured what stood out in the survey data. Each person in turn presented a picture and what it represented. Others in the dialogue could then respond in a constructive manner: "What I see in your picture is . . . and the way I might connect it to the challenges we face is . . ."

One picture was of a boy lying awake in bed. The person who chose this image saw comfort and recovery from illness. But others in the group saw fear in the boy's expression. An image of a farmer walking behind a plow also raised the topic of fear, as people said things like "We are so traditional. It can be frightening to break new ground."

The group had thus uncovered a troubling theme: fear was not uncommon at the hospital. But why fear? Where did it come from?

The hospital was managed to high standards. The middle managers especially had come to see themselves as primary owners of these standards, feeding a hyperresponsibility for success. Yet out of this management culture also came a strong sense of fear about even the possibility of censure and reprisal for any mistake. The CEO's invitation to take risks in the name of leadership seemed at odds with tight management.

One manager illustrated this cultural norm in a story of a nurse who was reprimanded for being five minutes late to a patient consultation meeting because she was ushering another patient and family to their room. The nurse was caught between the traditional hospital norm of "everything on time" and the new norm of "customer focus." She was afraid to do the wrong thing. A number of such stories led the group to ask themselves, "How do we handle these inevitable collisions between inventing new forms of customer-focused leadership and the strict professional management disciplines of running a hospital?"

Such feelings of fear were difficult to talk about in public. But others listened and sought to understand. The CEO in particular had to work through his reaction ("People are afraid of me . . . me?") and see his unique place in a hierarchical management culture that was perceived as paternal and threatening to innovation. Several examples of how this fear played out were discussed—quite gingerly at first. A new level of openness in the dialogue began to take shape.

An important step to making shared sense across the organization was the senior team's sharing the results of the dialogue with the organization. Instead of saying, "Here's our plan," it chose to invite the rest of the organization into a similar process. Some of the pictures from the dialogue were circulated, including a description of the issues they evoked. Often the reaction was "That's good work, and I want to be a part of it."

The process of using dialogue as a tool for shared sense making laid the groundwork for the bold actions required to become a customer-focused hospital. Hospital employees now say that they feel more "on the same page." The changing direction of the hospital makes more sense to them. Now they better understand and can deal with some of the strong emotions that had previously blocked progress. The effort has also deepened appreciation for the many positive things happening in the organization. ("You are doing great work! Don't be afraid!") The hospital's leadership initiatives are increasingly based in freshly explored shared values rather than short-term pressures.

The hospital is continuing these forums for making shared sense of the challenges it faces as an organization. An upcoming round of dialogue will have more people in it, including managers at every level from around the hospital. This next round will aspire to reach a new level of shared learning and integration. Where are the patients (customers) in the hospital's new sense of itself? Where are the doctors? Where are the local community leaders? How can these groups and others be included in the process of building shared understanding? The process outlined in Exhibit 2.9 will let you try a similar experiment.

Systems Thinking

Effective strategic thinkers are able to discern the interrelationships among different variables in a complex situation. For example, they might wonder what would happen to sales of a product if the price

---

**Exhibit 2.9. Suggestion for Development:
Making Common Sense.**

- Explore with others the strategic implications of alternative images or pictures of your future.
- Collaborate with others in a collective effort to represent your mission or vision using words or images.
- Have a dialogue with others about your strategy using stories or metaphors.
- Communicate your strategy using pictures, visual images, or other data displays.
- Ask questions of others' perspectives during conversations so as to deepen your understanding of their views.
- Express doubts or criticism in a constructive way.
- Collaborate with others in building new strategic perspectives.
- Hold a complex issue open to debate and deliberation without rushing to an answer.
- Create ways to discuss the undiscussable.
- Seek strategic insight with a sense of learning and curiosity by holding all possibilities loosely rather than as positions to be defended and debated.

---

to consumers was reduced. Or what would happen to sales if marketing was increased? If these variables operated in a simple linear fashion, then either choice would increase sales. But if they represented variables in a complex and dynamic system (as is more often the case), then the results would be less predictable. For example, if product quality was an important component of product attractiveness for consumers, then a decrease in price might be perceived as an indicator of poor product quality and consequently slow sales, no matter what was spent on marketing.

Systems thinking can help you better understand complex problems like these, so it's an important tool for your strategic thinking toolkit. The basic premises of systems thinking may seem a bit odd at first because they run counter to customary ways of thinking about things. If you try to practice the discipline of systems thinking, however, you might understand complex problems in new and helpful ways. In general, systems thinking is especially useful when *assessing where we are, learning how to get there,* and *checking our progress,* as depicted in Figure 2.5.

In this section we offer five tactics for better systems thinking that we emphasize in our DSL program. (The framework presented here has been adapted from an excellent treatment of systems thinking by Barry Richmond, 2000.)

- Look for patterns over time.
- Look at the big picture.
- Look for complex interactions.
- Hypothesize key causal relationships.
- Validate your understanding of "what causes what."

Long-Term Patterns. People's usual approach to things in most spheres of life can be characterized by what we call *static thinking.* With static thinking, attention and energy are focused on whatever the current crisis seems to be (a rising number of traffic accidents, for example, or decreasing profits or high employee turnover). Success tends to be defined in terms of solving that crisis (by decreasing the number of accidents, increasing profits, or reducing turnover).

This approach seems reasonable (or at least familiar), but there are two problems with it. One has to do with the path by which the current state was reached, and the other has to do with knowing the best path for getting from the current state to a more desirable one in the future. With static thinking, little attention tends to be given to "how we got here," and equally little attention tends to be given to "how we'll get from here to there."

Dynamic thinking, by contrast, examines how key variables brought a system to its present state (and may be keeping it there), and it uses understanding of the past to guide future initiatives. This emphasis upon understanding pathways is important, since undue focus on current conditions tends to be associated with assumptions of linear trajectories from the past to the present and

Figure 2.5. Strategy as a Learning Process: Systems Thinking.

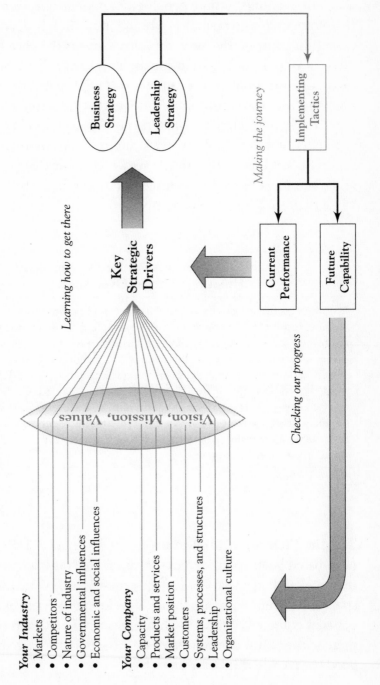

from the present to the future (for example, the number of traffic accidents went up because penalties for poor driving were too low; therefore, increasing penalties should immediately decrease accidents). In contrast, dynamic thinking assumes the path forward is often nonlinear rather than linear. This certainly is the case for many organizations. For example, solving tough organizational challenges often requires investments that take time to have an impact. There is often a short-term cost of some kind before a desired effect takes hold. It's not a straight line from investment to results. It is often true that things get worse before they get better—and sometimes, as in the example in Exhibit 2.10, they get worse while they look as if they're getting better.

Exhibit 2.10. Suggestion for Development: Charting Changes Over Time.

It is often useful to focus on relative indicators of performance rather than absolute indicators of performance. For example, a financial institution monitored several aspects of credit card use. It noted that the number of cardholders was increasing, total revenue was increasing, and the number of transactions was increasing. Everything was trending up, and that seemed good. But a group at this company then examined relative revenue measures. It discovered that dividing annual revenues by the number of cardholders produced a trend line that first curved upward but then curved downward. This suggested that the company was increasingly attracting marginal customers.

Source: Richmond, 2000.

The Big Picture. Catholic Healthcare Partners (CHP) is a large faith-based health care system. Its senior vice president for human resources and organizational effectiveness is Jon Abeles, who is responsible for, among other things, developing executives throughout that complex system. Jon himself is a big-picture thinker, but more to the point, he wants leaders throughout the system who are good big-picture thinkers themselves.

Within the population of upper management at CHP are executives who have strategic responsibilities at the facility level (within individual hospitals employing as many as a thousand people), some who have responsibility at the regional level (for many hospitals and encompassing up to eight thousand people), and some who have responsibility at the system level (ten regions encompassing forty thousand people). Abeles says he wants leaders who understand the big picture from their own vantage points in the system as well as from higher perspectives, and who can be strategic leaders of the whole system at whatever level they are assigned.

Such big-picture thinking involves seeing at each level how the different parts of a system operate as a whole (in CHP at the facility, regional, and enterprise levels). And big-picture thinking at each level is not possible using the detailed quantitative analysis of parts (functions, departments, divisions, silos, and so on) that is ubiquitous in organizations today. Barry Richmond puts it cogently: "Breaking things down into more detail and increasing numerical accuracy rarely provides the leverage needed to break a logjam in our thinking, identify a high-leverage strategy, or defuse resistance to an organizational change effort. Instead, what we need is exactly the opposite: more synthesis, more knitting pieces together so as to see new connections" (2000, p. 15). Exhibits 2.11 and 2.12 will get you started with big-picture thinking.

Complex Interactions. Consider the following question: Does positive organizational climate lead to good performance, or does good performance lead to positive organizational climate?

If you're having difficulty choosing between these alternatives, you're in good company. Seemingly reasonable arguments support each point of view. For example, if you belong to the climate-causes-performance school of thought, then you might point out that happy workers are productive workers and that positive feelings about the organization and coworkers foster effective coordination and support across departments.

Exhibit 2.11. Suggestion for Development: Raise Your Sights.
Elevate your perspective so you can rise above your immediate circumstances. A good way to do this is by finding where boundaries exist in your organization's environment. Boundaries may take the form of assumptions people make about a problem, about the work, or about the walls separating different teams, functions, or departments. ("Connected Leadership," a major new research-and-practice thrust within CCL, pursues the idea that many leadership challenges within organizations today involve the disconnectedness of different parts.) The task here is to practice taking a high enough perspective that boundaries recede (and perhaps new sorts of boundaries will emerge). Second, look for similarities rather than differences in the companies, people, problems, and so forth that you come across. Believe it or not, looking for similarities is harder than it sounds; humans are hardwired to notice differences (contrasts and contours, for example). But cultivating an ability to discern similarities amid superficial differences will help you see through to the essence of issues.
Source: Richmond, 2000.

On the other hand, if you belong to the performance-causes-climate school of thought, then you might point out that successful workers are happy workers and that strong performance validates the effectiveness of collective work and strengthens feelings of respect and confidence in coworkers.

Although positive climate and strong performance tend to be positively correlated, they usually have a more complex relationship than such linear thinking suggests. For example, if you believe that performance creates climate, then you might institute actions specifically intended to motivate performance, like additional incentives for exceptional performance (spot bonuses, for example). And you might be surprised if performance subsequently decreased, which could happen if introducing competitive rewards disrupted effective working relationships among employees.

Alternatively, if you believe that climate affects performance, then you might commit considerable employee time and energy

Exhibit 2.12. Suggestion for Development:
The Elevator Speech.

Craft an elevator speech about your organization's strategy (or what your division's, department's, or team's role in that strategy is). An elevator speech is so brief it can be delivered in just a minute or two, the duration of a short elevator ride. Its very brevity makes it a challenge; it isn't easy to identify what is central to say, and to say it clearly and succinctly. (As Mark Twain once said, "I would have written you a shorter letter, but I didn't have the time.") Many good leaders have found it a helpful practice to have several different elevator speeches always at their disposal, as need or occasion arises.

into meetings to find ways to improve organizational climate. And you might be surprised if you subsequently observed that organizational performance decreased following these meetings—not an unlikely outcome if employee energy has been distracted from production processes. Understanding that the appearance of simple causal relationships often masks complex interactions among unpredictable variables can alert you to the possibility of the unintended consequences of your actions.

Key Causal Relationships.   Strategy is about trade-offs: choosing to do this rather than that, choosing to be this rather than that, choosing to develop one capability over another. By its nature, a good strategy is not all things to all people. A good strategy is clearly centered on a few key priorities.

Determining what the key priorities are for your organization in your particular competitive environment is, of course, the challenge. Ironically, one aspect that makes it challenging is our ability to identify many different factors that all seem relevant to organizational performance.

For example, assume that your task is to identify corporate success factors in a manufacturing organization. You might identify a variety of factors: supply costs, manufacturing efficiency, product quality, marketing, product development, manufacturing capacity, product pricing, sales force effectiveness, brand strength, organizational structure and culture. Although each one might well play some part in overall success, it's unlikely that investing in them equally would be a wise strategy. The strategic challenge for any organization is to integrate understanding of its aspirations, strengths, and weaknesses with understanding of its competitive environment in order to identify the two or three critical leverage points that bring success. These are the key strategic drivers.

Understanding What Causes What. It's important for leaders in organizations to confirm their theory of the business. Of course, few people merely assume their organization is performing well; most look for signs or results to indicate they're leading the organization in the right direction. But there is a hidden danger in how leaders sometimes validate their search for signs, as the following story suggests.

In 2004, a tragic accident occurred on a Colorado highway (Associated Press, 2004). Three people were killed when a forty-ton girder fell on their car from an overpass under construction. What made the accident even more tragic was that a passing motorist had spotted the girder's precarious position on the overpass earlier and reported it to the state patrol. The motorist, experienced in bridge construction himself, indicated that the girder "just didn't look right." A transportation crew was dispatched to investigate the situation, and it coincidentally discovered a downed sign in the middle of the highway in the general vicinity of where the problem had been reported. The crew told authorities that the problem could be repaired later and then left, believing it had discovered the problem that the motorist had reported and that it did not require immediate attention. The crew looked no further, so never saw the precarious beam that had prompted the motorist's call.

This kind of thinking is such a common source of error that it's been given a name: *confirmation bias*. People, including leaders, have a tendency to look for information that will confirm what they believe (or "know to be true") rather than to look more intentionally for information that could disconfirm their preconceptions. The danger in organizations is that if people look only for signs that they are on the right path (that their theory of the business is valid), they can often find them. But if they do not also look for signs that they are wrong, they will miss critical information.

This kind of thinking error was studied by P. C. Wason (1960), a psychologist who asked college students to guess the rule he had used to develop a particular three-number sequence: 2-4-6. To check their understanding of the rule, he had them generate their own sets of three numbers; Wason would then tell them whether or not their sets conformed to his rule. They could test as many different number sets as they wished, and when they felt confident they knew the rule, they were to announce it.

By the time the students announced their answers they were never in doubt, but they were seldom right. Typically they formed some erroneous hypothesis (for example, counting by twos), and then searched for information that would confirm it. Since Wason's actual rule was "any three ascending numbers," their own three-number sequences always conformed even though they misunderstood the rule itself. Similar research also suggests that people are much more likely to seek evidence that will verify their thinking than evidence that might refute it. Exhibit 2.13 is an exercise in theory development and testing.

How Strategic Thinking Relates to Acting and Influencing

This chapter has focused on strategic thinking, one of the engines that drive strategy as a learning process in organizations. The next two chapters focus on the other two engines, strategic acting and strategic influencing.

Before beginning Chapter Three, however, we should note again, as we did in Chapter One, that strategic thinking is not an entirely separate process from strategic acting, nor from strategic

Exhibit 2.13. Putting Theory to the Test.
First, identify some specific and testable implication of your current theory of business. Then determine what kind of result or data would be consistent with that implication. Also try to identify what data or result could disconfirm it.

influencing either. Take, for example, the strategic thinking skill of making common sense. It certainly involves thinking, but the modifier *common* implies a communal nature. It involves making sense together, not just within your own head. The essence of the skill is to create in a collaborative way a common and shared understanding among different individuals with different perspectives, not to issue an edict.

Making common sense involves the interaction of strategic thinking and strategic influencing as well as the interaction of different individuals. Larry Bossidy (Bossidy & Charan, 2002) made a similar point in emphasizing the importance of constructing and sharing a common picture of what's happening inside and outside an organization. Doing so, he said, requires a "social software" in which debate and negotiation take place, but in ways that are more collaborative and creative than adversarial. When this happens it represents the interaction of thinking and influencing—and ultimately of strategic acting too—that lies at the heart of effective strategic leadership. We believe that execution, the discipline at the core of Bossidy's book, is basically about this interaction of strategic thinking, acting, and influencing.

Chapter Three

Strategic Acting

Strategic thinking and strategic acting have a close connection to one another and to strategic influencing. In most organizations, translating strategic thinking into priorities for action is one of the most challenging aspects of strategic leadership. Strategic acting is important in every aspect of strategy as a learning process, but it is a critical part of *learning how to get there, making the journey,* and *checking our progress* (see Figure 3.1).

Many factors make it difficult to translate strategic thinking into action. As noted in Chapter One, these factors include the lack of clear strategic focus, the difficulty of aligning tactics with strategy, and the difficulty of integrating short-term objectives with long-term ones. To transform thinking into action, strategic leaders must be ready to act in the face of uncertainty. They must set clear priorities, act with short- and long-term interests in mind, and allocate resources that match the strategic choices the organization makes. They must create conditions under which others can be effective, including ways they and others can learn from their individual and collective actions.

The Nature of Strategic Action

It's one thing to have a strategically compelling idea. It's quite another to take action based on that idea. In part, that's what Lee Iacocca meant when he said, "If I had to sum up in one word what makes a good manager, I'd say decisiveness. You can use the fanciest computers to gather the numbers, but in the end you have to set

Figure 3.1. Strategy as a Learning Process: Focus on Action.

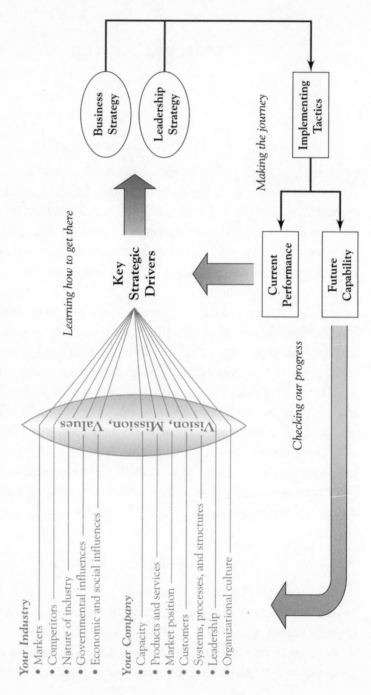

a timetable and act" (1984, p. 50). But Iacocca only told half the story here. He captured one kind of tension between thinking and acting: the kind when prolonged thinking delays action. Another kind can occur when perpetual action precludes critical thinking.

Here's what we mean. Most managers probably feel as though they spend most of their working day in an acting mode. We don't mean playacting or pretending, but rather that they are constantly doing something: making decisions, taking a call, hurrying to one meeting after another, finishing almost-overdue reports, and so on. If you're like most of the managers and executives we work with, the demands on you for action of one kind or another may seem so incessant that you find precious little time for thinking.

In this sense you are, like those other managers, acting all the time. Managers and executives, often by both their roles and dispositions, are busy people. But our focus in this chapter is not on all forms of acting; it's on the more specific idea of strategic acting: *committing resources to build sustainable competitive advantage*. This is the kind of decisive action that is consistent with the strategic direction of the organization, that leaders carry out despite the ambiguity, complexity, and chaos inherent in organizational life.

Examples abound: Which of several new product possibilities should receive the greatest share of development resources? Where should you place your marketing emphasis—on developing existing markets or new ones? Which new project will offer the greater long-term advantage? Whom do you appoint to lead the new corporate innovation team? What stand should your company take with regard to questions being raised about its environmental impact? So long as questions like these are merely under consideration, strategic thinking is involved. But when resources are committed—money, time and energy, personal or corporate reputations—strategic acting comes into play.

Does this mean that every action is a strategic action? No. Just as not all leadership is strategic, not every action is strategic. The critical issue is whether it's reasonable to expect an action to have an impact on the organization's sustainable competitive advantage.

Selecting the next manager of the company mail room is not likely to have a strategic impact on the organization, nor is choosing one vendor over another to supply catering services. But selecting someone for the organization's new chief learning officer position probably will.

The rest of this chapter examines six general competencies that make up strategic acting:

- Set clear priorities.
- Create conditions for others' effectiveness.
- Make strategy a learning process.
- Act decisively in the face of uncertainty.
- Act with the short term and the long term in mind.
- Have the courage of your convictions.

Before we turn to those competencies, however, it might be helpful for you to complete a brief self-assessment of your own strategic acting skills (see Exhibit 3.1).

Set Clear Priorities

In Chapter Two we noted that certain facets of strategic thinking tend to be relatively underdeveloped and underutilized among managers and executives despite their potential value. That applies here too. While most managers and executives are fairly skilled in what we might term the rational aspects of decision making, the nonrational aspects of strategic decision making pose quite a challenge. You can see a common example of this in how spouses might have quite different perspectives about priorities for the family's finances. One might feel strongly that more money needs to be put away for a rainy day while the other believes more should be spent to address current needs and desires. When feelings and values impact decisions, it does not necessarily make decisions irrational, just nonrational. There's a big difference.

Exhibit 3.1. Evaluate Your Strategic Acting Skills.

For each of these behaviors, use the following scale to assess your need to improve in that area.

1	2	3	4	5
Considerable Improvement Needed		Moderate Improvement Needed		No Improvement Needed

Be decisive in the face of uncertainty.

1   2   3   4   5

Manage the tension between success in daily tasks and success in the long term.

1   2   3   4   5

Implement tactics consistent with strategy.

1   2   3   4   5

Make decisions that are strategically consistent with each other.

1   2   3   4   5

Facilitate others' actions by providing them a helpful balance of direction and autonomy.

1   2   3   4   5

Find ways to reward appropriate risk-taking.

1   2   3   4   5

Recognize the need to adapt existing plans to changing conditions.

1   2   3   4   5

Learn from actions by deliberately reflecting on their consequences, and use such learning to inform future decisions and actions.

1   2   3   4   5

Examine mistakes for their learning value (as opposed to apportioning blame).

1   2   3   4   5

Setting clear priorities is one of the most important things strategic leaders do. Setting priorities facilitates coordinated action across the enterprise, and it also provides a basis for acting decisively with the short term and the long term in mind. Of course, priorities can change and sometimes circumstances necessitate exceptions to the general rule. Nonetheless, decision making about allocating resources is easier when you know the relative importance of the different possibilities. Setting priorities is particularly important during the *learning how to get there* element of strategy as a learning process, which we've highlighted in Figure 3.2.

It confuses people when leaders publicize key organizational priorities but then put more resources into other things. It also frustrates people when leaders send unclear signals by communicating, in essence, that everything is important.

Another common example of unclear priorities occurs when costs must be cut. Does the organization's leadership implement, for example, across-the-board 15 percent cuts in each functional area, or does it differentiate among those that represent greater and lesser strategic priority for the organization and allocate resources accordingly?

The latter alternative is less common but more strategic. It requires differentiating between alternative ways of allocating scarce resources in terms of their relative contributions to the organization's future vitality. All managers and executives deal with supply-and-demand challenges: they face more demands for resources than they have available, whether the resources are dollars, bodies, or time. The organization needs to invest more in marketing, for example, but it also needs more sales staff. It needs to invest more in product development, and it also needs new IT systems. It needs to improve quality control in its manufacturing processes, and it also needs to create more competitive compensation packages to attract talented people to its technical staff. The trade-offs go on and on.

Setting clear priorities will be easiest and have the most enduring impact when people throughout an organization share a common understanding of what three or four factors are contributing most to its long-term success. In Chapter One we introduced the

Figure 3.2. Strategy as a Learning Process: Setting Priorities.

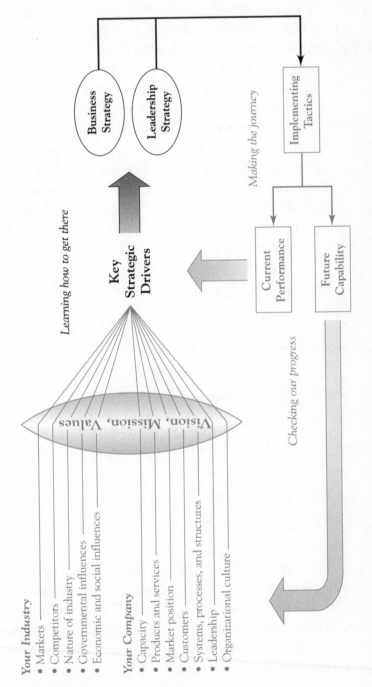

Assessing where we are

Understanding who we are and where we want to go

Your Industry
- Markets
- Competitors
- Nature of industry
- Governmental influences
- Economic and social influences

Your Company
- Capacity
- Products and services
- Market position
- Customers
- Systems, processes, and structures
- Leadership
- Organizational culture

Vision, Mission, Values

Learning how to get there

Key Strategic Drivers

Business Strategy

Leadership Strategy

Implementing Tactics

Making the journey

Current Performance

Future Capability

Checking our progress

idea of *strategic drivers:* the relatively few factors that any given company considers most important to building and maintaining sustainable competitive advantage. Most organizations have no more than a handful of these drivers, and these represent a select few among the larger population of factors on which companies in an entire industry compete. Thus one of the key decisions for any organization is the selection of strategic drivers on which it will competitively differentiate itself from others in its industry.

Doing so helps set priorities with regard to resource allocation: which two or three aspects of your business merit the most resource allocation, if the goal is to maximize the company's sustainable competitive advantage? The list of candidates for greater invest-ment is long in any organization, and often includes alternatives such as these:

- Changes in product pricing
- Changes in customer service staffing
- Enhancement of product development efforts
- Reduction of product development cycle time
- Changes in manufacturing capacity
- Changes in manufacturing efficiency
- Enhancement of quality
- Changes in sales force size
- Changes in sales force compensation
- Changes in marketing

Getting clarity about these priorities, or key strategic drivers, is only the beginning. It's still necessary to determine a specific strat-egy based on these priorities. And still more priorities must be set to guide decisions about the organizational culture, structure, and systems needed to implement the strategy effectively, especially if it represents a major change.

Avoid Mixed Signals

Some leaders undercut their own effectiveness by sending mixed signals. This can happen in a number of different ways. You have probably observed some of these common instances:

- A leader thinks out loud (without noting it as such), and some people take such words as a call to action but others do not.
- A leader doesn't "walk the talk." The leader's actions and words are inconsistent, for example, emphasizing the importance of cost-consciousness to everyone else yet not applying the same frugality to personal expenses.
- A significant gap opens between espoused strategy and strategy-in-practice (or between deliberate and emergent strategy).
- A leader highlights "key organizational priorities," and yet goes on to put more resources into other things.

Some leaders don't differentiate among competing priorities at all, implying that everything is a priority. In such cases, others will be left to their own devices to know what's important, and poorly aligned actions are nearly inevitable. Exhibit 3.2 suggests a way to see whether you've sent mixed signals.

Exhibit 3.2. Getting Feedback.

Ask for candid feedback from one or two of your more trusted and astute colleagues (ideally your direct reports). Find out whether they recall specific times when you have sent mixed messages to them or others, and if so, precisely what it was that you did that confused others as to your intent.

Assuring Strategic Alignment at Xerox

During the past three years, CCL has worked with Xerox Corporation in developing what we believe is a best practice in assuring strategic alignment among executives across all corporate functions and lines of business. This successful initiative depended upon the interplay of strategic thinking, acting, and influencing.

In 2002 Xerox held five "Executive Strategy Alignment Workshops" for its top executives worldwide, drawing as many as seventy-five participants at each of the sessions. The purpose of the workshops was to achieve common vision and endorsement for Xerox's new corporate strategy among its top three hundred executives. That goal was to be achieved through

- Assuring consistent understanding of the new corporate strategy, business imperatives, and financial picture
- Translating the new strategy into its implications for organizational leadership
- Agreeing on what changes in current organizational practices were required to make the new strategy successful
- Providing a forum for two-way communication and feedback about the strategy and its implementation between the executive team and the top executives worldwide

In addition, the workshops were intended to prepare those top leaders to cascade the strategy to their employees. Each of the workshops followed a similar format. For half a day the executives, who came from all functions and lines of business, listened to presentations about the new strategy by various members of the Xerox management committee. For the rest of the day they were divided into diverse seminar-size groups of about fifteen. Each group addressed a common set of questions about the strategy and reached consensus about the most critical responses to each. These were the questions:

- What excites you about the strategy?
- What concerns you about it?

- What barriers to successful implementation need to be addressed?
- What questions or comments do you have for the CEO or other members of the top team?

Following these group discussions, members of the management committee, including CEO Anne Mulcahy, visited each of these groups to listen to each group's summary and to answer questions. This format was very popular with the executives in that it allowed relatively personal and open dialogue about evolving corporate strategy and its implementation with the corporation's top leaders. It was followed two years later by a similar workshop (slightly different in format in that it involved all three hundred top executives meeting in one session) with similar success.

Jim Firestone, Xerox's chief strategist and president of the company's corporate operations group, described the process this way:

> The purpose of these workshops was to create proactive, hands-on sessions where our leadership community could engage, ask questions, push back, and raise issues that impeded their ability to execute. Open discussions around the implications, issues, and requirements for implementation enable leaders to deal with conflict and ambiguity and to make the right decisions toward a common goal. Our sessions in 2002 gave us feedback on areas we needed to work on and provided our executives with what they needed in order to cascade and implement the strategy in each of their organizations. When we revisited the process again two years later, we shared with the management team the progress we made as a result of their feedback from the first session.
>
> Alignment is one of the most important steps in successful strategic change. Nothing is more powerful for creating alignment and commitment than openness and responsiveness. At Xerox, we were successful in engaging the right people to help influence and implement a solid strategy that is delivering impressive business results.

Managing Strategic Priorities at Starbucks

Facilitating coordinated action across the enterprise requires knowing what initiatives represent the most important strategic priorities for the organization at any given time. Unfortunately, what seem like priorities to one person may not seem like priorities to another. Some short-term requirements are important to attend to, but without strategic clarity it's difficult to determine which are more important than others. Starbucks is an excellent example of how an organization can identify priorities for strategic action.

Starbucks is one of the most recognizable brand names in the United States and is becoming increasingly so around the world. It has grown from its inception in 1971 as a single retail store in Seattle to become the dominant retailer of specialty coffee in North America, with more than eight thousand stores worldwide.

Being a dynamic and high-growth organization has obvious advantages, but it also presents distinctive challenges. One of them is having numerous competing priorities, which can inhibit a company's ability to execute things well and to focus its resources and energy on the right things at the right time.

Helping Starbucks set those priorities was Margaret Wheeler's responsibility when she was manager of prioritization alignment and calendaring for the company's retail operations in North America. Wheeler served as an "air traffic controller" for any type of activity that occurred in the North American business unit. More specifically, she played a key part in translating the company's strategic objectives into prioritized action. After strategic objectives were set and key programs identified to drive those strategic objectives, her team took over to provide a road map for translating that high-level strategy into action.

One important element of the process involved realistically assessing how much capacity the organization had for new initiatives. How many new projects could it take on during the course of any given year and execute effectively from the perspective of the operating field stores? For example, how many new beverages could

Starbucks successfully introduce in a year? How many learning initiatives could be introduced—and done well?

Wheeler's North American leadership group met twice a month to review all the organization's initiatives at the start of their development. The group provided a final answer to the question: Will we roll this out? Complicating this decision-making process were the inevitable unplanned opportunities that arise and require resetting priorities. The organization's reaction to Wheeler's group was positive because this decision-making process allowed people throughout Starbucks to focus on actions that would make the most difference at any time.

Create Conditions for Others' Effectiveness

Thus far our attention has primarily been on setting priorities in the business strategy portion illustrated in Figure 3.2. It's also important to set clear priorities about how the business strategy will be carried out—priorities that deal with the human and organizational capabilities needed to implement the business strategy effectively (see Chapter Six for a more in-depth examination).

Balance Direction and Autonomy

Today's competitive environment involves ever-increasing uncertainty, complexity, ambiguity, and pace of change. That's why agility is such a prized organizational capability these days—it takes agility to compete in this kind of environment. Agility is also prized because it's a difficult organizational capability to master. It runs counter in many ways to long-standing notions about how organizations need to operate to be successful. Hierarchical command-and-control authority structures and detailed formalization and standardization of policies and procedures used to be the norm in organizations. Most organizations did operate effectively with those structures and procedures in relatively stable and predictable environments, but few organizations face those conditions today.

Strategic leaders today must create conditions for others' effectiveness commensurate with these new competitive conditions. The challenge now is to balance the need for structure and predictability with the need for decisiveness and action, to balance the structure and predictability of a strategic plan (or alternative plans, appropriate to different potential future scenarios) with the need to be decisive and take the action required to achieve strategic objectives. Exhibit 3.3 offers ideas about how you can review the balance between direction and autonomy in your own organization.

Reward Appropriate Risk-Taking

One of the major barriers to decisive action in the face of uncertainty is the tendency of an organization (or a particular senior leader) to make punishments for mistakes more impressive than rewards for achievement. This was a particularly strong factor in the case of one large manufacturing company we worked with. Time and again, its executives described this sort of dynamic as part of their culture. They all agreed that it was far more beneficial for any manager's career in this organization to set relatively low strategic targets and then exceed them than to set significant stretch targets but barely miss them. Managers got bad marks if they just missed an ambitious stretch target and good marks if they achieved a lowball safe target even if the actual performance level (measured, for example, by sales revenue) was higher in the "just missed" case. The executives we talked to all recognized how this cultural norm distorted target forecasting and possibly even suppressed actual performance (it was politically unwise to develop a reputation for chronically poor forecasting), but they seemed helpless to change so powerful a norm in so large a company.

Even if you can't change the culture of the whole organization, like the executives in our example, you can take steps to change the culture and behavior of people in your part of it. It is important to do what you can do where and when you can do it. As a strategic leader you can create protected space for prudent initiative and

Exhibit 3.3. Direction and Autonomy.

It's important to strike an appropriate balance between the need for direction and the need for autonomy. This exercise has two parts. In the first part you'll identify what a more optimal balance between these might be for your organization. In the second part you'll learn an approach for identifying actions to change in the desired way.

Part 1: Determining the Current State

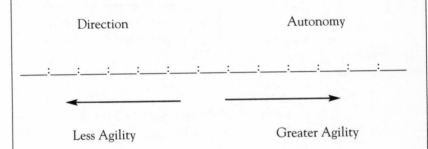

On the Direction-Autonomy continuum, place an A in the space representing the actual state of affairs in your group. Then place an O in the space representing the optimal state of affairs for your group. The relative placement of the A and the O will give you a rough idea of how much change toward greater or less agility will be optimal for your group.

Part 2: Identifying Change Opportunities

In this part you'll use a process called Force Field Analysis. It's a way of depicting the opposing forces that maintain any particular current state of equilibrium, and thereby identifying potential actions for moving the current equilibrium point in the desired direction. Typically a Force Field Analysis depicts desired change as moving toward the right. Here's an example of what a Force Field Analysis looks like. For the purposes of illustration we'll assume this case involves desired change toward greater agility.

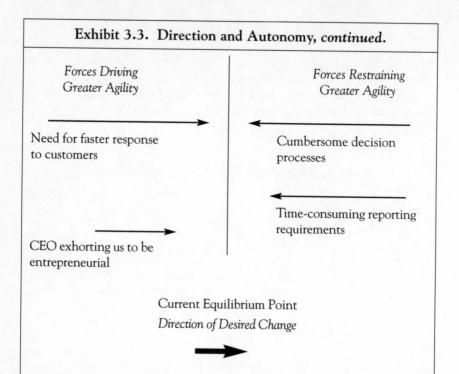

Exhibit 3.3. Direction and Autonomy, *continued.*

Forces Driving
Greater Agility

Forces Restraining
Greater Agility

Need for faster response
to customers

Cumbersome decision
processes

Time-consuming reporting
requirements

CEO exhorting us to be
entrepreneurial

Current Equilibrium Point
Direction of Desired Change

Using Force Field Analysis

1. State the present situation and the desired situation.

2. Illustrate the present equilibrium in terms of a vertical line represented by the convergence of two sets of arrows. Arrows pointing to the right will represent forces promoting desired change and arrows pointing to the left will represent forces restraining desired change.

3. Use brainstorming to identify the forces promoting and restraining desired change.

4. Evaluate each force in terms of both the impact of changing it and the ease of changing it.

5. Starting with the most easily changed and highest-impact forces, develop strategies to reduce restraining forces and increase promoting forces.

risk-taking by those who report to you, even if you may not enjoy that freedom yourself.

Of course, like most managers, you probably believe that you *do* reward appropriate and reasonable risk-taking. But it's just as important to avoid punishing or discouraging reasonable risk-taking. It may seem self-evident at first that rewarding appropriate risk-taking means, by definition, not discouraging it, but the issue is more complicated than that. That's because of the importance of differences in point of view. Much depends on the eye of the beholder.

To put it differently, you may be able to point to things you've said or done to specifically reward appropriate risk-taking. Others, however, may see it differently. They may even see ways in which, from their perspective, you've actually stifled it. So the extent to which you encourage appropriate risk-taking ultimately must be determined on the basis of the impact of the totality of your behavior on others. In that regard, it's useful to consider a broader set of behaviors than whether after the fact you believe you've rewarded appropriate risk-taking. (Exhibit 3.4 provides some useful factors to review.)

Starbucks Revisited. Margaret Wheeler's story at Starbucks is an excellent example of how strategic thinking and strategic acting go hand in hand, and it's also a good example of strategic initiative coming from the middle of an organization. It was Wheeler's insight that the task she'd been given—getting the calendar of initiatives in order—was in some ways the wrong task; she recognized the challenge was really about strategic priorities. As she explains, "We started with a very small, specific mission, which was to fix the calendar. Now, two years later we've come up with a decision-making and prioritization process linked to strategic planning. No one told us to do that. We uncovered an organizational need, and there were a lot of people who were really supportive of it and who wanted to make things better aligned, and we were able to do that."

Exhibit 3.4. Measuring Capacity for Risk.

Here are some questions you can use to explore the broader climate and context of risk-taking within your group or team.

- Are we encouraging an appropriate level of risk-taking for us to be successful?

- What are some examples of appropriate risks that we've taken in the past?

- What are some examples of seemingly appropriate risks that we didn't take?

- Are there any patterns in those two sets of examples?

- Are there certain kinds of risk that we need to be more prepared to take?

- Are the criteria clear about when taking a particular kind of risk is appropriate?

- How do we handle mistakes? Does the response to failure stifle even moderate levels of risk-taking?

- How much risk-taking takes place "under the radar"? Would it be better if we had a better handle on the actual level? What would that take?

- When we know an action was successful, do we also know the degree of risk taken to achieve that success?

- How well do we use examples of risk-taking with both positive and negative outcomes as teaching opportunities for shared learning and development?

- How safe do people feel that they won't be punished for taking what appeared to be a reasonable risk, if it eventually goes south?

- What barriers have we imposed on ourselves that constitute obstacles to appropriate risk-taking?

- What can the leader do more of (or less of) to encourage appropriate risk-taking?

Margaret Wheeler clearly deserves credit for the initiative she took, but so does Starbucks—for having created a climate that encourages that kind of initiative.

Make Strategy a Learning Process

Making strategy a learning process requires a particular mind-set as well as distinctive behaviors in each element of the process. The foundations of making strategy a learning process, however, are set in the formulation of leadership strategy, as highlighted in Figure 3.2. This is typically the work of strategic leadership teams as well as individual strategic leaders.

Test Organizational Theories

As we've discussed, an organization's business strategy can be thought of as its theory of what it takes to be successful. Over time, organizations accumulate data relevant to the usefulness of that theory and on the validity of particular expectations and experiments (tactical business decisions, for example).

When viewed this way, strategy as a learning process seems to begin with strategic thinking. Strategic thinking generates hypotheses that are subsequently tested through strategic action. But as we have seen, simple causal relationships are not always what they appear to be or the whole story. In this case, learning also can occur if strategic acting precedes strategic thinking. In fact, the iterative nature of thinking and acting makes identifying the starting point somewhat arbitrary. The crux of the issue is how to test strategic thinking with acting and how to learn from action that has been taken.

When business tactics are thought of as hypotheses by which business strategy is tested, tactics have two related purposes: the obvious one is execution, but another is learning. Perhaps not surprisingly, organizations tend to deemphasize the role of tactics in service of learning because that purpose is less appreciated.

That's one reason why it's useful to see strategy as a top-down and a bottom-up process. Strategy needs to be set at the top, but it also needs to be informed by the insights of others throughout the organization. If it is not, it is apt to be seriously flawed. As Andrew Campbell and Marcus Alexander (1997) noted, "Separating strategy formulation from implementation generally is not a good idea. Most of the insights important for strategy formulation reside in the heads of the operating managers" (p. 48). Henry Mintzberg (1987) coined the term *crafting* strategy to reflect the dynamic ways managers in the field act strategically in adapting to new opportunities and threats as they arise.

As Campbell and Alexander (1997) noted, however, "Tactics are not only about implementing today's strategy but also about discovering tomorrow's strategy." Their view is consistent with understanding strategy as a learning process. This can be seen in Figure 3.1, in the way the results of implementing tactics provide feedback loops that inform current performance as well as future capability. For these feedback loops to work optimally, part of the task of determining tactics should involve addressing the question of how they can be designed to collect data relevant to informing future strategy.

Conduct Business Experiments

Here is an example of appreciating the value of using tactical decisions to enhance potential learning. An executive in a media company had been given responsibility for a qualitatively significant if financially modest corporate diversification. Part of his challenge in making the case for diversification was to demonstrate understanding of the strategic drivers in this unfamiliar business. He was by nature quite innovative and entrepreneurial, and he looked forward to implementing a great variety of tactical decisions. A colleague, however, advised him to be more scientific by curbing his natural impulse to try everything in his choice of tactics. The colleague suggested that the executive would not be able to reach a clear conclusion if he changed every variable with every different test, and advised that he choose something specific and vary it systematically.

This collegial advice to deepen strategic insight is supported (unbeknownst to the helpful colleague) by research into management practices associated with successful, discontinuous innovation (breakthrough, revolutionary innovation rather than that based on incremental improvement). Researchers have found, for example, that although conventional forms of market research are useful in guiding incremental change, they have limited impact on more radical kinds of innovation. Of far greater value is what the researchers termed a *probe-and-learn* process. This process amounts to a series of market experiments and the introduction of prototypes into a variety of market segments (Lynn, Morone, & Paulson, 1996). Early versions of products are introduced (probing), and insights gained from market reactions to that probing (learning) guide continuing product development. For example, Motorola introduced its first handheld cellular telephone in several cities in 1973, ten years before fully commercial systems were sold. While the early prototypes generated relatively little interest, they did provide Motorola with valuable market insight. For example, it learned those versions were too bulky and heavy, and size and weight became critical design factors for several decades.

The probe-and-learn process suggests that the way to assess the strategic viability of an idea or opportunity is, literally, to pursue it—to introduce an early version of a product or service, learn about the market and technology, and then modify the offering based on that learning. While the process has much to recommend it, however, it nonetheless should be used selectively. It reduces strategic uncertainty—but at considerable cost. No company could pursue this approach—or sustain the process over many years—with more than a small fraction of potential opportunities. It is best suited to opportunities for discontinuous innovation that are strategically central to the enterprise.

The exercise described in Exhibit 3.5 invites you to conduct your own business experiment.

Exhibit 3.5. Find a Strategic Initiative.

Identify a new initiative you could launch to take advantage of changing competitive conditions while helping to sharpen your own senior leadership's strategic vision and insight. Now think about it as a business experiment. What strategically useful lessons could you learn from the initiative's success? Its failure? What kind of data would you need to collect that would be relevant to validating your experiment?

Learn from Your Actions

One way of doing this is with an after-action review (AAR). An AAR is a systematic method of learning from your actions. The U.S. Army developed the procedure, and it has been adopted and adapted by civilian organizations. The focus is on performing better in the future by capturing key insights quickly and then translating them back into action. It's about becoming more action oriented, not more analytical. And it is not about fixing blame on individuals or teams. It won't work in an environment of fear. An AAR has six key steps (Baird, Holland, & Deacon, 1999).

1. *What was the intent?* What was the action's intended outcome or purpose? What was to be accomplished, and how was it to be accomplished?

2. *What happened?* What were the results, and what events contributed to them? Who were the critical parties, what were the critical communications, and what other critical junctures or connections were revealed? (One way of getting at this information is by asking key participants or stakeholders to reconstruct events chronologically. Another is to ask stakeholders what the key events were and then probe deeper for clarifying information.)

3. *What was learned?* What's known now that wasn't known before? What lessons learned will help someone else do better next time?

4. *What actions should be taken?* Based on the lessons learned, what should be done? What can be done to produce immediate benefits? What can be done to affect systems, policies, and practices? What can be done in the long term to affect strategies, goals, and values?

5. *Take action.* The whole idea of an AAR is doing something with what's been learned.

6. *Disseminate the findings.* Make sure others who might benefit from this learning are made aware of it.

Analog Devices is a high-tech company that has applied the AAR process in its product development teams. The impetus was the company's recognition that too much time and too many resources were being wasted because little to no learning was taking place across the different teams; teams were making the same mistakes over and over again. Table 3.1 illustrates the format used by Analog product development teams. It shows examples from one semiquarterly business review meeting and may give you an idea of how you could adapt the process to your own organization.

Act Decisively in the Face of Uncertainty

Strategic leadership means acting decisively in the face of uncertainty. This can be difficult for many reasons, including these:

- Changing conditions make it difficult to accurately assess the risk-reward ratio of an action.
- Failure of an initiative carries potential risk to one's own career, department, or entire organization.
- Organizational cultures or formal and informal reward systems sometimes discourage risk-taking.
- It is tempting to reduce uncertainty by investing in safer bets, even if the payoff may also be commensurately less.
- Action imposes opportunity costs of not pursuing other options.

Table 3.1. The Semiquarterly Business Review (AAR) at Analog Devices.

Step 1	Step 2		Step 3	Steps 4+5	Step 6
Intent	*What Happened? Why?*		*Lessons Learned*	*Action*	*Dissemination*
Objective	What happened?	Why did this happen?	What are the implications?	What are the lessons learned?	Who, what, and when?	Who needs to know?
Start correlation and final test board.	Not started.	Unrealistic estimate by team leader.	Unmet expectations.	Get buy-in from team members for schedule estimates.	Jack and Sue to update schedule for Test Dev. by 1/18. Jack and Sue to "start" correlation of Final Test board by next SBR.	Team leader.

Complete debug of XYZ board.	Completed on schedule.	John worked lots of overtime.	Stress. Any unplanned problems would have pushed out schedule since we are already working max hours. No buffer.	Should have allowed more time in schedule to complete this task.	Review all trims to accommodate package parameters.	Schedule builders.
Release trim.	Trim not released.	Sam T. is multiplexed between too many tasks.	Sam will continue to run production trim for #1 if trim is not released. Sam will not focus on #1 if he continues to be distracted by other projects.	Release of program is jeopardized without focused resources.	Release #1 trim by 2/1.	Sponsors, team leaders, Sam's manager.
Deliver fully functional units to customer in June.	Package cracks identified during engineering look-ahead.	Assembly engineer performed test prior to package qual.	Package being redesigned.	Perform engineering look-ahead tests on new package.	Results of package redesign due late May by assembly engineer.	Other team leaders.

Source: Adapted from *Organizational Dynamics*, (27, 4), Baird et al., page 28, copyright 1999, with permission from Elsevier.

Strategic Decisions Always Involve Uncertainty

Factors like those listed above notwithstanding, effective strategic leaders do act in the face of uncertainty. That's not to say they don't do everything possible to reduce the uncertainty. It just means that perfect certainty is unattainable (and maybe not even desirable), and so action cannot wait for perfection. What's more, not only does the formulation of strategy occur amid uncertainty but the enactment of strategy does too. Some of the most important opportunities for acting decisively in the face of uncertainty occur while *learning how to get there* and *making the journey,* as highlighted in Figure 3.3.

One dramatic example of decisions in the face of uncertainty was American General Dwight D. Eisenhower's decision (on June 5, 1944) to send the largest amphibious force in military history across the English Channel and begin the liberation of Europe from Nazi Germany. He had already postponed the invasion because of adverse weather over the channel, and the weather remained bad. Another postponement would mean further delay of not just days, but weeks or months. In weighing his options, Eisenhower knew that the invasion's success was anything but certain. Weather reports indicated some chance of a break in the storm, but no certainty that it would last long enough for reinforcement units to get ashore in France. Finally, after getting input from everyone assembled, he announced his decision to invade with a terse "OK, we'll go" (Ambrose, 1983).

What gives certain leaders the confidence to take bold strategic action when the outcome is uncertain? Marilyn O'Connell, vice president of marketing for Verizon's retail markets, gave some insight into that sort of executive judgment. Verizon was facing a strategic decision concerning the deployment of fiber-optic cable. One side of the decision equation was well known: the cost to deploy the cable. What was not knowable was what capabilities the deployment of the fiber would enable over the next ten to twenty years. Thus the strategic decision became a matter of judgment:

Figure 3.3. Strategy as a Learning Process: Acting Without Certainty.

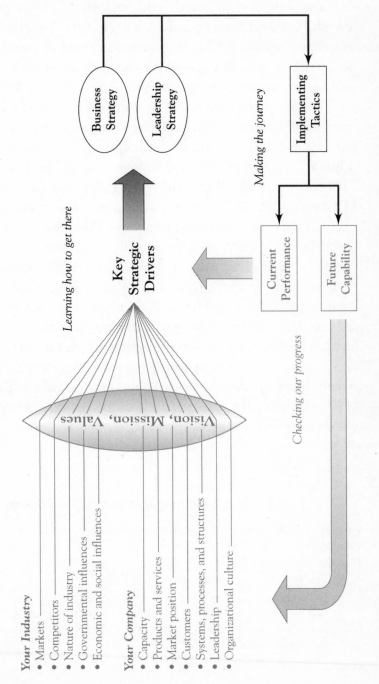

Assessing where we are

Understanding who we are and where we want to go

Your Industry
- Markets
- Competitors
- Nature of industry
- Governmental influences
- Economic and social influences

Your Company
- Capacity
- Products and services
- Market position
- Customers
- Systems, processes, and structures
- Leadership
- Organizational culture

Vision, Mission, Values

Learning how to get there

Key Strategic Drivers

Business Strategy

Leadership Strategy

Implementing Tactics

Making the journey

Current Performance

Future Capability

Checking our progress

Would Verizon be able to solve problems in the future and develop the capabilities it would need in the future to make the investment feasible? O'Connell said it boiled down to this: "Do I believe we'll figure this out later?" But you can't wait until later to make the decision. She said, "If you always look at what you know and what you've always done in the past, you will never do anything."

Thus far, we've been referring to uncertainty in a fairly general way. Perhaps it would be helpful here to become more specific about just how much uncertainty is acceptable when making strategic decisions. Ultimately, of course, that's an unanswerable question. There are too many other variables to suggest a simple formula, but in his autobiography, *My American Journey*, Colin Powell described his own approach to decision making: "The key is not to make quick decisions, but to make timely decisions. I have a timing formula, P = 40 to 70, in which P stands for probability of success and the numbers indicate the percentage of information acquired. I don't act if I have only enough information to give me less than a 40 percent chance of being right. And I don't wait until I have enough facts to be 100 percent sure of being right, because by then it is almost always too late. I go with my gut feeling when I have acquired information somewhere in the range of 40 to 70 percent" (1995, pp. 380–381). The exercise described in Exhibit 3.6 will help you clarify your own decision-making tendencies.

Exhibit 3.6. Analyzing Your Strategic Decisions.

Review specific strategic decisions that you made in the past. For each one:

- Briefly identify the decision.
- Recall as best you can the different sorts of factors you weighed in making the decision. Try to estimate the subjective probability you had at the time that your actions were right (that is, would produce a successful outcome).

- Recall the process you went through (for example, data collection, discussions with others, and so on) by which you were ultimately ready to act or decide.
- How frequently did your action or decision fall within the 40 to 70 percent range that Colin Powell recommends?

Now look at any strategic decisions that you are facing now. For each one:

- What is your subjective probability *now* that an action or decision in this case will be correct or successful?
- If you are above the 40–70 range, have you delayed the decision unnecessarily?

Assessing the Level of Uncertainty

Some organizations face less certain competitive conditions than others. An article in *Harvard Business Review* (Courtney, Kirkland, & Viguerie, 1997) describes four levels of uncertainty, and different strategies are appropriate for each different level.

- *Level 1* is called a "clear-enough" future because there is enough strategic certainty for managers to develop a single forecast that is precise enough for strategy development. For example, companies developing a strategic response to a competitor's move in a relatively mature industry are in this situation.
- *Level 2* is called "alternate futures" because the future can be described in terms of a very small number of discrete scenarios. For example, companies facing possible regulatory or legislative control are in this situation.
- *Level 3* is called "a range of futures" because numerous outcomes are possible along a continuum defined by key variables, as distinguished from the few discrete scenarios found in Level 2. Companies in emerging industries are often in this situation.

- *Level 4* represents true ambiguity. So many factors are
  interacting to create uncertainty that the future is nearly
  impossible to predict. Fortunately, this situation is quite rare
  and relatively transitory, as conditions tend to migrate to
  one of the other levels over time.

You might try to identify which level best characterizes the
level of uncertainty your own organization faces.

Act with the Short Term and Long Term in Mind

Strategic acting requires attending to long-term as well as short-
term objectives. In Chapter One we referred to this as a distinction
between strategic leadership and operational leadership, and it's
highlighted in Figure 3.4. Acting with both the short and long
term in mind is an important part of *learning how to get there, making the journey,* and *checking our progress*.

Data that we've collected from more than five thousand members of teams in organizations indicate that this can be a challenging
tension to manage effectively. About 20 percent of the respondents
on a CCL survey that assessed the effectiveness of organizational
teams disagreed with the assertion that an appropriate balance had
been struck between dealing with short-term and long-term needs
(see Chapter Five for a closer look at strategic leadership teams).
While this data pertains specifically to perceptions of team effectiveness in balancing short-term and long-term needs, it's consistent with
what we hear from managers in general about how difficult this balancing act can be. Jack Welch put it this way: "I always thought any
fool could do one or the other. Squeezing costs out at the expense of
the future could deliver a quarter, a year, maybe even two years, and
it's not hard to do. Dreaming about the future and not delivering in
the short term is the easiest of all. The test of a leader is balancing the
two" (2003, p. 124).

The challenge is not just in having the discipline to invest in
the future and the present. It's also in having a strategy that is clear

Figure 3.4. Strategy as a Learning Process: Acting with Time in Mind.

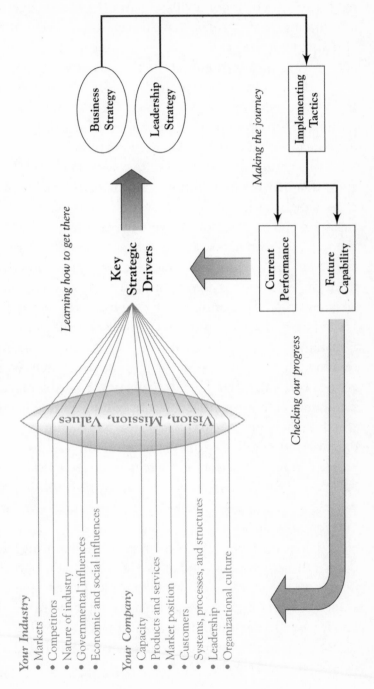

Assessing where we are

Understanding who we are and where we want to go

Your Industry
- Markets
- Competitors
- Nature of industry
- Governmental influences
- Economic and social influences

Your Company
- Capacity
- Products and services
- Market position
- Customers
- Systems, processes, and structures
- Leadership
- Organizational culture

Vision, Mission, Values

Key Strategic Drivers

Learning how to get there

Business Strategy

Leadership Strategy

Implementing Tactics

Making the journey

Current Performance

Future Capability

Checking our progress

to people in the first place. In our survey we also asked about the extent to which respondents' organizational strategies were discriminating, so that people have a clear sense of what they will do and also what they will not do. A quarter of the respondents disagreed with the assertion that their strategies were clear.

Without strategic clarity and focus it is nearly impossible to make wise decisions about tactics. The exercise described in Exhibit 3.7 invites you to think about what it will take for your own organization to succeed in the long term.

By its nature, investing in future capability often means investment that may not demonstrate immediate results. Many organizations launch key initiatives that never seem to gain foothold or lead to lasting and meaningful change—in part because their leaders do not stay committed to strategic purposes and ends. With regard to the quality movement, for example, research indicates that investments in TQM can pay off significantly only when the investment is significant and enduring over a time frame of years, not months.

While perhaps the most obvious example of acting decisively is making a decision, it can also be reflected in consistent and determined support of key strategic priorities over time. Welch's own actions epitomize that. He talked about the need for focus and for passionate commitment around those long-lasting initiatives by which leadership tries to change the fundamental nature of an organization. "I followed up on [those initiatives]," he said, "with a passion and a mania that often veered toward the lunatic fringe" (2003, p. 298). Welch was clear about the few most important priorities for GE's success, and he stayed the course—and made sure everyone else did too.

Strategy is about clarity of focus; it's about knowing what not to do as well as what to do, and understanding that the what not can be just as important as the what to. It facilitates decisions about what not to get into in the first place, and it facilitates decisions about when to get out of things. At a tactical level, it facilitates decisions about what projects or programs to launch and what projects or programs to stop.

Exhibit 3.7. Envisioning Capability.

Imagine your organization (department, division, or whatever) one or two years from now. What new or stronger capabilities would significantly enhance your organization's effectiveness? What investments (financial, technical, human) should you be making now to enhance your capabilities in the future?

During Welch's early years as CEO of GE, his seemingly draconian personnel cuts—a quarter of the company's staff left the payroll within five years of the time he took on the position—earned him the nickname "Neutron Jack." (A neutron bomb is one that kills people but leaves buildings standing.) Welch said the nickname hurt, but he also hated the bureaucracy and waste in GE at the time. Despite his nickname and despite once being named the Toughest Boss in America, Welch now feels that he actually did too little too late. He says, "The ironic thing was that I didn't go far enough or move fast enough. When MBAs at the Harvard Business School in the mid-1980s asked me what I regretted most in my first years as CEO, I said 'I took too long to act'" (2003, p. 132).

Finally, it's important to remember that acting with the short term *and* the long term in mind involves not just deciding what future investments need to be made but also what present assets need to be preserved. Isabel Swift, a vice president at Harlequin, commented on the paradoxical difficulty posed by the strength of all her company's lines of business. "One of our challenges," she said, "involves redirecting and growing an organization that is actually quite successful." An important part of that success is because of readers' familiarity with the brand, so one of Harlequin's strategic challenges is to maintain the promise of the brand while still growing it and changing it. "The power of that brand is very precious," she said, "and we don't want to walk away from it."

There are many approaches to assuring strategic alignment within an organization, and most include measures or metrics by which the organization assesses its performance. In Figure 3.1, this refers to the phase of strategy as a learning process that we call *checking our progress*. Checking progress is important, but such metrics also represent more than an after-the-fact performance scorecard. By their nature, key metrics also direct organizational efforts toward some ends rather than others.

That's why it's so important to assess current performance and future capability, or what we've referred to previously as operational results and strategic results. This helps assure that all units are pulling in the same direction—and that it's the right direction for the organization's long-term sustainability.

Selecting the right metrics to assess current performance and future capability is one of the most important things you can do as a strategic leader. Here are a few things to keep in mind as you do so. First, in keeping with the idea that strategy is about making choices, it's important to have a relatively small number of key metrics. That's because your key metrics should be based upon your strategic drivers, of which there should be no more than a handful; you might have one or two metrics for each driver. Second, these measures ought to hang together as a logically integrated expression of organizational strategy. Oftentimes organizations develop metrics that merely represent a diverse array of measures, mistakenly believing this qualifies as a balanced scorecard (Kaplan & Norton, 1996). This often leads them to use too many strategic measures. The problem is that the very act of identifying many strategic measures usually reflects a lack of clarity about those relatively few things (strategic drivers) that are most critical to enduring organizational success.

The other problem occurs when a variety of measures are selected without due consideration of their logical relationship to an overall integrating strategy. If a scorecard merely represents an assortment of different sorts of measures independent of their logical relationship to each other and an overall strategy (they just seem like good things to measure), then the net effect on the organization could be to pull it in different directions. It would decrease effort and dilute rather than leverage success.

It's helpful to approach the identification of key metrics with the objective of putting the chain of reasoning underlying business and leadership strategies to an empirical test. Therefore, since these strategies are ultimately intended to help assure sustainable competitive advantage, it is vital to examine how you are doing now (this quarter's sales, for example), as well as how effectively and wisely you are investing in the future capabilities most critical to your enduring success (for example, investment in research and development, or evidence that you're attracting and retaining top talent). One approach to identifying these critical future capabilities is described in Exhibit 3.8 at the end of the chapter.

Have the Courage of Your Convictions

Earlier in this chapter we looked at Eisenhower's decision to launch the D-Day invasion amid uncertainty over its success. A measure of that uncertainty—and of Eisenhower's character as a leader—is that even as the ships and planes were heading to Normandy, he penned an apology to the people of the Allied nations, taking full responsibility himself for the invasion's failure. Fortunately, that letter was never needed.

Typically, however, immediate feedback about the wisdom and outcome of strategic decisions is the exception rather than the rule. Investing in future capabilities inherently involves investing in uncertainties, and the validity of those investments may not be clear for months or years or, in some cases, even decades. Thus it takes strength and courage to stay the course of investing in future capabilities when other investments may also seem attractive—and to some, perhaps, more attractive.

When Darwin Smith became CEO of Kimberly-Clark, its primary business was producing coated paper. Its greatest assets, understandably, were its paper mills. Smith became convinced, however, that Kimberly-Clark's future lay in becoming a paper-based consumer products company, not a paper producer. Based on that conviction, he sold the company's paper mills. At the time, it was considered a foolish and reckless move by virtually everyone outside Smith's own team. Over many years, however, Smith's insight and conviction were validated (Collins, 2001), and Kimberly-Clark is now the leader in its industry.

On a different scale, you may also be facing decisions about what future capabilities are most important to invest in—about what future capabilities you are willing to commit to and stay committed to while the ultimate outcome of those investments remains uncertain. Strategic leadership requires acting in the face of uncertainty and a commitment to stick with those investments over time, born of conviction that those investments are building greater future capability.

How Strategic Acting Relates to Thinking and Influencing

The competencies covered in this chapter highlight the close connection between strategic thinking and strategic acting. For example, the value of clear priorities is greatest when they are derived from good strategic thinking. In the first two chapters we emphasized the importance of identifying key strategic drivers, those relatively few leverage points most critical to enduring organizational success. *Identifying* those drivers depends, among other things, on systems thinking. But identifying them isn't enough. It's just as important to use knowledge of those strategic drivers to set priorities for allocating resources. Strategic thinking and strategic acting go hand in hand.

In a similar vein, the advisability of decisive action in the face of uncertainty depends largely upon the quality of strategic thinking brought to bear on the situation. That would require having scanned the environment to accurately understand the organization's current strategic situation, including the opportunities and threats you're facing in the external environment. It also typically requires bringing others into the process for making common sense of the situation. And decisive action in the face of uncertainty is only likely to serve constructive ends if it is grounded in a deep understanding of the complex variables involved—systems thinking.

The value of systems thinking also applies to acting with the long term as well as the short term in mind. It presumes a deep understanding of those relatively few factors critical to an organization's enduring success, not just to its current performance. Again, strategic thinking and strategic acting go hand in hand.

It should be equally clear that strategic acting is also closely connected to strategic influencing. For example, creating conditions for others' effectiveness is *all about* influencing others. So is acting to make strategy a learning process. The whole point of both these competencies is to influence people throughout an organization to act individually and collectively in ways most likely to build sustainable competitive advantage.

It's appropriate, therefore, to turn our attention now to a more detailed look at the third key element of strategic leadership—strategic influencing.

Exhibit 3.8. Measuring Future Capability.

How do you measure capabilities necessary for future success? Not surprisingly, the first and most critical step is to identify what they are. But that's not a simple matter. Here's one approach that involves having a structured conversation among key stakeholders to identify your organization's key strategic drivers.

This exercise works best when between six and twelve people participate, each having a deep and distinctive perspective on the organization's operations and competitive situation. It usually takes half a day to work through this five-step process.

1. Spend several minutes individually brainstorming specific things you believe are critical to drive the organization's long-term competitive success. They can include current capabilities, whether effective (and needing to be maintained) or ineffective (and needing to be improved) or currently nonexistent (and needing to be developed for future success). Strategic drivers can be a skill or talent, a competitive capability, or a set of conditions a company must achieve. They can relate to technology, marketing, manufacturing, distribution, and organizational resources.

2. Identify which four or five of those in your judgment are the most critical to future success whatever their current state of effectiveness. Write each of these on a separate note.

3. Post everyone's notes (each person's top four or five) in a large common area (for example, on a large white board or on a presentation easel), and as a team begin sorting individual notes into affinity groupings. For example, those dealing with product development might be sorted into one group. This process typically leads to between eight and twelve distinct groupings.

   a. Sorting the notes into affinity groups is more of an art than a science. It's important for your team to have a shared understanding of what each grouping means, and it's important for each grouping to represent as specific a driver as possible. For example, a cluster of notes categorized as "leadership in product development" is usually more helpful than a broader and more heterogeneous grouping dealing with the general area of "innovation"; a cluster of notes categorized as "attract and retain top talent" will be more helpful than one dealing with "strong people programs."

   b. Involving everyone present in this sorting process is critical. Determining these categories is one example of the strategic thinking skill of making common sense. It involves creating shared understanding about what each of the various groupings means (and what they do not), not superficially designating some shorthand label for each grouping that might be interpreted differently by each person present.

c. Moving some notes from one cluster to another, creating new clusters, and renaming clusters are all natural as the discussion proceeds and the team refines its understanding.

d. Often there will be a few notes that never do align well with any groupings. Keep them "alive" nonetheless, and don't assume they're less important just because the issue was identified on only one or two notes. Sometimes just one person initially identifies what ultimately proves to be a key strategic driver.

e. One of the most common errors during this process is to confuse strategic drivers with desired outcomes. A strategic driver is best thought of as something you can invest in; an outcome is not. For example, increased market share might be a desirable outcome, but what would you invest in to achieve it?

4. When you've agreed upon a final set of potential drivers, the next step is to discuss and assess the relative importance of each one with every other, in turn.

a. It helps if the discussion is framed in a fairly precise way. Ask this question for each pair of alternatives: If you could invest in only one of these two, which one is more critical to assuring sustainable competitive advantage for the organization? (For the time being, don't worry about relative costs between the alternatives.)

b. Each person present should make a forced-choice vote for one alternative or the other in every possible pairing. In almost every pair of alternative drivers, there will be some people who see one alternative as more important and some who see the other alternative as more important.

c. When everyone is ready to vote, count and record the number of votes each alternative receives. This will be easier if you prepare a matrix with each alternative appearing in both the rows and columns of the matrix. In each appropriate cell, put the number of votes received by the item in the respective row when it is paired with each different item in every column (see, for example, Appendix A).

5. These votes will ultimately lead to a rank-ordered list of key strategic drivers. But that's not yet the basis for measuring the capabilities

Exhibit 3.8. Measuring Future Capability (*continued*).

needed for future success. Ultimately you'll want to focus on the two or three drivers representing patterns combining the highest relative importance and lowest current effectiveness. These will be the drivers for which you will develop metrics to assess for future capability. Here's one way of identifying those drivers:

a. As a whole team, go down the rank-ordered list of key strategic drivers. Rate each driver on a 1-to-5 scale, indicating your judgment of the organization's current effectiveness in using it to drive sustainable competitive advantage (1 = nonexistent or not effective at all; 5 = extremely effective).

b. When you have completed these effectiveness ratings, identify the two or three drivers that are most important to your future strategic success and that the organization is presently least effectively (or not at all) implementing.

c. These are the drivers that will need substantial investment before their potential contribution to long-term success can be realized. By definition, they're unlikely to demonstrate attractive returns in the short term. During this period of driver investment, therefore, use metrics that reflect your buildup of that capability.

Chapter Four

Strategic Influence

Strategic influence is how leaders engender commitment to the organization's strategic direction and learning. It is absolutely essential to sustaining competitive advantage in contemporary organizations. But the complex, chaotic environment in which organizations operate makes it difficult for their leaders to set a plan, get others on board, and implement a strategy in some lockstep fashion. Organizations and the people in them must adapt and learn on the fly. Leading them through strategic influence is a never-ending quest.

Like any quest worthy of the name, it is rife with challenges. Strategic leaders often know the path to pursue (through their strategic thinking) and might be decisive and confident enough to walk that path despite the uncertainty (through the courage of strategic acting), but enlisting others in the effort can be much more difficult. It is often the most critical element of building sustainability.

When asked, "What challenge do you personally face to being a better strategic leader?" about 17 percent of the executives attending CCL's Developing the Strategic Leader program specifically discuss the challenge of gaining endorsement of and commitment to their ideas. Some executives describe how difficult it is to influence others over whom they have no authority. Still others talk about the difficulties of influencing large groups of people—many of whom they never address on a one-to-one basis. Another common challenge is influencing in all directions: down to direct reports, laterally to peers, up to bosses, and outside the organization. Yet, faced with these different challenges, the leaders we work with share one realization:

strategic leaders can't achieve success all by themselves; success requires the committed efforts of many.

For anyone working to become a strategic leader, developing and using strategic influence involves forging relationships inside and outside the organization, inviting others into the process, building and sustaining momentum, and purposefully utilizing organizational systems and culture. It demands that leaders be clear about what drives them, be able to see and understand other perspectives, and, paradoxically, be open to influence from others.

Because strategic work operates between individuals and groups and crosses functional lines, influence skills become even more important. In cross-functional groups, people may not see eye to eye on things, particularly if they have conflicting goals. Becoming a strategic leader requires that you pay attention to the political landscape defined by function and power. It asks you to create common understanding—between yourself and others, and among others. To answer that challenge, you must use the power of language to help people interpret information in ways that are helpful to the long-term success of the organization. You must develop with others a consistent message and deliver it in ways that acknowledge the value of others. You must celebrate successes large and small to build and sustain momentum. You need that forward movement to propel the organization through the learning cycle.

Strategic Influence

Just as not all leadership has strategic implications, not all influence is strategic in nature. Consider, for example, a team in a design engineering firm that comes together to work with a client, assess its needs, and create a design for that client. The team's goal is to deliver its service in a high-quality fashion. Mutual influencing among the members of the team invariably takes place; for example, one person may try to persuade another that some adjustment to the schedule might be appropriate in light of a change request from the client. That might well be an important change to make for the work to be successful, and while this success is important to the design firm, we would not say it's of strategic importance to the firm. But suppose those same individuals happen to be on a team considering a change in their business model. For example, suppose this organization considered itself in the business of selling a product (the "design," for example), and now it is beginning to think about the value it provides to clients as a service (the "design process," for example). The nature and quality of their mutual influence in a situation like this clearly has strategic implications for them, and so we would consider it strategic influence. On a more general note, influence is strategic when it is exercised in service of the long-term success of the organization. That is, it is strategic influence when it is exercised in service of the strategy-making and implementation efforts that are depicted in the framework of strategy as a learning process, shown in Figure 4.1.

It often involves influencing other parts of the organization and even those outside the organization. For example, the strategic leader may exert influence to achieve the following types of outcomes:

- Get people on the same page regarding a long-term strategic direction.
- Engender buy-in from people for a strategic venture so that there will be true commitment to it, not mere compliance (or worse, active or passive resistance).
- Significantly shift the way resources are being deployed or invested in line with strategic intent.
- Share insights and observations with more senior executives relevant to the strategy's viability, effective implementation, or capacity to match competitors' moves.

Influence and the Strategy Process

One way to think about strategic influence is to consider how influence relates to the learning process shown in Figure 4.1. When executives work together to assess where they are, influence plays

Figure 4.1. Strategy as a Learning Process: Influence at Every Phase.

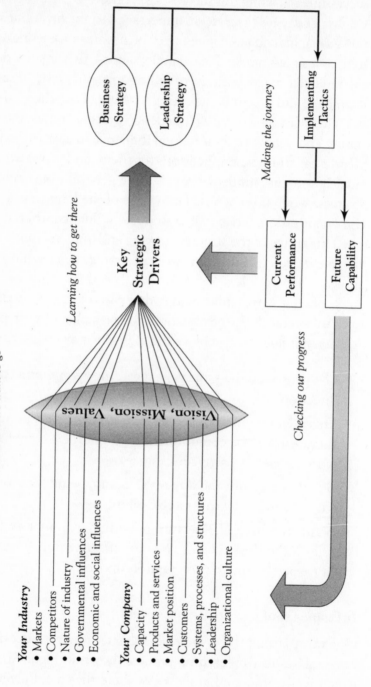

Assessing where we are

Understanding who we are and where we want to go

Learning how to get there

Your Industry
- Markets
- Competitors
- Nature of industry
- Governmental influences
- Economic and social influences

Your Company
- Capacity
- Products and services
- Market position
- Customers
- Systems, processes, and structures
- Leadership
- Organizational culture

Vision, Mission, Values

Key Strategic Drivers

Business Strategy

Leadership Strategy

Implementing Tactics

Making the journey

Current Performance

Future Capability

Checking our progress

a critical role. As Floyd and Wooldridge (1996, p. 69) note, "The kind of understanding of strategy that develops within organizations is significantly affected by how managers influence each other's perceptions of the strategic situation," so effective influence here clearly has implications for the organization. Consider, for example, the task of doing a SWOT analysis. To the extent that the group doing that analysis is open with one another and members feel free to look at strengths and weaknesses honestly, the SWOT might or might not be productive. How unfortunate it can be for the organization if one of the leaders in the group has a critical strategic perspective but cannot influence the rest of the group to see that point of view.

Influence is also core to *understanding who we are and where we want to go*, as the purpose of this element is to identify and hold true to a purpose for the organization. Influencing a change in the mission, vision, or values of the organization is quite difficult, as these elements define the identity, or the core, of the organization. In Chapter Three we discuss the decision of Darwin Smith, CEO of Kimberly-Clark, to change from a paper business to a paper-based consumer products business (Collins, 2001). This decision necessitated the sale of some paper mills that were an integral part of the Kimberly-Clark history and identity. In a sense, he was changing the company's core—what everyone thought would always be true about Kimberly-Clark. Clearly, Smith faced a huge strategic influencing task.

In the strategy process, organizations must also engage in *learning how to get there* through an exploration of their strategic drivers, and by setting business and leadership strategies to satisfy those drivers. We discuss in preceding chapters the importance of focus and collaborative learning in these efforts. Focus implies that some efforts in the business may be seen as more important to the organization's success than other efforts.

Executives typically carry around implicit business models in their heads about what factors cause success, and different executives have vastly different implicit models. Unfortunately, they can't all be right. One might approach influence here from a win-lose perspective: "If I influence better than you do, my role in the organization will be more powerful than your role." Or even more pragmatically, "If I influence better than you do, my budget won't be cut." Again, how unfortunate it can be for the organization if scarce resources are not spent wisely simply because one or two key people are excellent influencers. So influence here must be in the context of collaborative learning to co-develop deeper business insight—that is, to make common sense. To do that, strategic leaders must be very clear about what is important to them as individuals (for example, by asking themselves, "To what extent do I view myself as a leader of my unit rather than a leader of this organization?") so that they are aware of any biases they might bring to the process. Additionally, strategic leaders need to balance their influence attempts with their own openness to accepting influence.

Influence when *making the journey* involves making sure people understand the strategy and how their work fits into it. It also involves keeping people on track when potential distractions arise, whether those distractions are external to the organization (for example, a move by a competitor) or internal to the organization (for example, a downsizing). During this phase of the strategy process, the strategic leader typically emphasizes efforts to build and sustain momentum.

Finally, consider the influencing power of various measures in your own organization. What key measures do you track? How were they chosen? In what ways are they (or aren't they) aligned with your strategy? As organizations and strategic leaders strive to accomplish the *checking our progress* step, they must pay careful attention to ensure that they are using the few best measures possible. The executives we work with frequently discuss the notion that you get what you measure. So a critical element of influence for a strategic leader is to ensure that the right measures are used in the right ways to look at both current performance and future capability.

The Multiple Directions of Strategic Influence

As strategic leaders move through the learning process framework, strategic influence must be exercised in all directions: up toward more senior executives, laterally toward peers in the organization, down to direct reports, and even outside the organization toward customers, analysts, suppliers, and others. In fact, gaining skill in influencing in all these directions is absolutely critical, as each of these stakeholders is essential to the strategic success of the organization.

Influencing upward is a necessary yet delicate art. Subordinate-level executives and managers have information and perspectives that are important for their superiors to hear, particularly because those lower in the organization are often closer to the customer. But someone who exercises strategic influence upward is attempting to change the direction that might have been set by those same individuals in the first place. It's an easier task when senior managers open themselves up to be influenced by asking for different perspectives and seeking input from those throughout the organization, but this does not always happen. Later in this chapter, we discuss the importance of establishing and maintaining credibility as a critical component of strategic influence. This component is particularly important when one is attempting to influence senior executives in the organization.

Influencing one's peers is also delicate. Strategic leaders are frequently acutely aware of the competition that can exist between peers: competition for resources in the organization, for attention, for power, for praise, and for the next promotion. So influence attempts can be met with skepticism and mistrust. Later in this chapter, we discuss the importance of building trust as part of engendering "unnatural" relationships. Building trust between peers is particularly important for strategic influence to be successful.

At first glance, downward strategic influence may seem to be the easiest. After all, isn't it true that all you need to do to influence your direct reports is to tell them what you want? From that point of view, you might not even think of downward influence as strategic at all insofar as it might involve the implementation of strategic initiatives. If influence is to be mutual, however, then methods of downward influence should not undercut the kinds of relationships in which two-way communication is enhanced. Similarly, helping people understand the strategy to see how their work fits into that strategy and the long-term success of the organization is critical. Later, we discuss specific ways to do this by involving others in the process and by connecting with them at an emotional level.

Finally, a strategic leader who is working to ensure an organization's sustainability in the environment cannot ignore the importance of influencing that environment. The environment includes any stakeholders with an impact on the organization: customers, suppliers, strategic partners, community, governments and regulating bodies, analysts, even competitors. Executives might consider their organization's relationship with the external world as more reactive, such that their job is to be the most agile reactor to what is happening in the environment. While that certainly is true, it is limiting to think that an organization cannot reach out and influence its environment. Consider, for example, the impact various government regulations can have on an industry. If organizations do not attempt to influence those regulations, they can suffer.

Strategic influencing clearly plays an important role in every element of strategy as a learning process. We now turn our attention to the competencies that are critical for strategic influencing. (These influencing competencies apply to every element of strategy as a learning process, so we don't highlight relationships between specific competencies and specific elements as in the preceding two chapters.) In some cases, these competencies might be demonstrated differently in the different directions of influence. So we will use a variety of examples and suggestions for development to point out some of the subtleties associated with influencing in different directions. Before we begin, take this opportunity to assess your own strategic influencing capabilities with the exercise described in Exhibit 4.1. We also recommend that in addition to rating yourself, you ask some of your

Exhibit 4.1. Evaluate Your Strategic Influencing Skills.

For each of these behaviors, use the following scale to assess your need to improve in that area:

1	2	3	4	5
Considerable Improvement Needed		Moderate Improvement Needed		No Improvement Needed

Understand your impact on others and how that affects the quality of collective work.

1   2   3   4   5

Build a network of relationships with people who are not part of the routine structure of your work.

1   2   3   4   5

Accurately assess the political landscape.

1   2   3   4   5

Navigate the political landscape without limiting your credibility.

1   2   3   4   5

Develop a compelling vision.

1   2   3   4   5

Create enthusiasm and understanding about a vision of the future in the hearts and minds of others.

1   2   3   4   5

Create ways to discuss the undiscussable.

1   2   3   4   5

Ask questions of others' perspectives to deepen your own understanding of their view.

1   2   3   4   5

Understand the needs, styles, and motivations of others, and use that information to communicate with them and influence them.

1   2   3   4   5

Exhibit 4.1. Evaluate Your Strategic Influencing Skills (*continued*).

Create champions throughout the organization to further your project or cause.

| 1 | 2 | 3 | 4 | 5 |

Use aspirational language and stories to draw people to your concepts.

| 1 | 2 | 3 | 4 | 5 |

Celebrate and advertise successes to build and sustain momentum.

| 1 | 2 | 3 | 4 | 5 |

Be open to influence from others.

| 1 | 2 | 3 | 4 | 5 |

---

colleagues to give you anonymous feedback on the same items, since effective influence is often best judged by others.

Developing Your Strategic Influence Capability

What does it take to engender commitment to the strategic direction of the organization? What does it take to bring others along as the organization learns more about that strategic direction? Most executives would attest that it takes more than a logical argument to get others on board. Logic might help you know you are right, but being right isn't always enough.

People often think of influencing in terms of persuasion: you have an idea or point to make, and it takes some particular interaction or series of interactions with people to persuade them to see it your way. Your thoughts frequently focus on others:

- What are they thinking?
- Will they agree with my ideas?
- What objections might they raise?
- What do they hope to accomplish?

- What piece of my thinking will be new for them?
- What are they hoping to hear?

Influence is actually different from persuasion. Influence does not often happen in one interaction. Rather, influence between two or more people is built, over time, on a solid platform of credibility and relationships. This platform forms the foundation of possible influence between people and groups, as shown in Figure 4.2. It is particularly important when the stakes of influence are strategic in nature.

Influence uses techniques to bring others along and then build upon that platform. In this chapter, we address the tactics that we believe are most fundamental to strategic influence, and also those least developed by the executives with whom we work. Not surprisingly, the tactics we address are also those that move beyond the logical arguments so many executives focus on when influencing.

Finally, strategic leaders must realize that influence does not stop when they get the yes. The scope and breadth of strategic change require attention to building and sustaining momentum for the process. As shown in Figure 4.2, this momentum carries the strategic initiative forward.

Let's begin our exploration of how to influence strategically by examining the foundation that must be built.

Start to Influence Others by Looking at Yourself

Being successful in the strategic influence process requires that people trust you. That is, by allowing themselves to be influenced, they are changing their beliefs, attitudes, and behaviors in ways that you request. They must trust your competence, your motivations, your style; and they must trust that you are going to take them and the organization to a place that is better than where they are today. Developing and maintaining that level of trust are critical to building a strong foundation of influence. You need to know your own

Figure 4.2. Components of Strategic Influence.

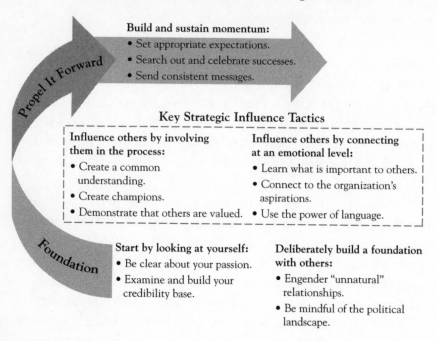

Propel It Forward

Build and sustain momentum:
- Set appropriate expectations.
- Search out and celebrate successes.
- Send consistent messages.

Key Strategic Influence Tactics

Influence others by involving them in the process:	Influence others by connecting at an emotional level:
• Create a common understanding.	• Learn what is important to others.
• Create champions.	• Connect to the organization's aspirations.
• Demonstrate that others are valued.	• Use the power of language.

Foundation

Start by looking at yourself:
- Be clear about your passion.
- Examine and build your credibility base.

Deliberately build a foundation with others:
- Engender "unnatural" relationships.
- Be mindful of the political landscape.

motivations and what is important to you, and closely examine your perceived credibility.

Be Clear about Your Own Passion. Sometimes we move through life and work trying to accomplish tasks but not necessarily thinking through, knowing, and feeling the importance those tasks have to what is important to us. That feeling of importance and commitment is passion, or conviction. It allows us to persevere in the face of adversity, and when others see this conviction, it can become infectious. In this section, we emphasize the importance of being excited and passionate about the work you do (see Exhibit 4.2). Later, we talk about engendering that excitement in others.

In Chapter One, we discuss the several roles that clarity about strategic drivers plays in facilitating an organization's success. Most important, that clarity provides focus for the many efforts of people

---

Exhibit 4.2. Understanding Your Passions.

Start by understanding the focus of your convictions and passion. Think of yourself as a person, not just an embodiment of your particular role or job. Explore where your passion lies by considering the following:

- What is the future you are personally hoping to achieve?
- What does it look like?
- What is exciting about that future for you?
- How does it fit with your personal values and aspirations?
- What kind of impact are you hoping to make in your lifetime?
- How do you define *success* for yourself, personally?

Now spend some time thinking about what is important to you in your work, from many different perspectives. For example, consider the following questions:

- What are your own personal values for work? What is important to you regarding the ways in which your organization succeeds, how people work together, the roles various people play, and so on?
- What future state are you trying to reach for the organization? What will it look like? Consider using the writing exercise from Exhibit 2.6 (in Chapter Two) to clarify your own personal vision for your work, whether it be for the organization overall or for a particular project you are working on.
- How does your vision for your work match up with your personal aspirations for yourself? What connections do you see?

---

in the organization, so that those efforts can be as effective as possible. In an analogous way, being clear about your own passions provides that same focus and intensity for you as a strategic leader. The clarity helps you to know which challenges to tackle. It also gives you the basis from which to get excited and energized about the work you are doing, and the persistence to spread that excitement to the rest of the organization. In Chapter Three, we discuss Jack Welch's passions, which "often veered toward the lunatic fringe" (Welch, 2003, p. 298). It's difficult to get on that "lunatic fringe" if you don't feel passionate about your work.

Examine and Build Your Credibility Base. "A platoon leader
doesn't get his platoon to go by getting up and shouting and saying,
'I am smarter. I am bigger. I am stronger. I am the leader.' He gets
men to go along with him because they want to do it for him and
they believe in him" (Item 182, 1960, p. 684). These words of
Dwight D. Eisenhower speak to the importance of credibility in the
influence process. When Eisenhower commanded the Allied troops
in Europe during World War II, even his greatest critic and neme-
sis on the British side, Field Marshal Bernard Montgomery, said of
Eisenhower, "His real strength lies in his human qualities. He has
the power of drawing the hearts of men toward him as a magnet
attracts the bit of metal. He merely has to smile at you, and you
trust him at once" (Montgomery, 1958, p. 484).

Influencing others strategically is virtually impossible if you
don't have credibility. Credibility involves two broad dimensions:
expertise and character. By *expertise*, we mean technical competence as well as organizational and industry knowledge, and the latter two are particularly important when thinking about strategic
leadership. Building organizational and industry knowledge requires
looking beyond one's specific job boundaries and responsibilities and
taking an enterprise-wide perspective. Without willingness and ability to do so, one's chances of influencing others strategically are significantly diminished.

The second component of credibility involves building trust in
your character and integrity. Studies of religion and philosophy, literature, business and government ethics, and psychology (Zauderer,
1992) have identified many behaviors central to a leader's integrity,
including these:

- Demonstrating concern for the collective good
- Truthfulness
- Fulfilling commitments
- Fairness
- Accepting responsibility

- Respecting others
- Celebrating others' successes
- Developing others
- Confronting unjust acts
- Forgiving others
- Extending self for others

It is also worth considering what specific behaviors can compromise one's integrity and credibility in the eyes of others. That's the focus of the questionnaire about trust in Exhibit 4.3 (adapted from Zauderer, 1992).

Although building credibility is important for any leader who is trying to exercise influence, it is particularly important for a leader who is attempting to influence people in higher-level positions. In our discussions with senior executives, they have told us that it is imperative to be known as someone who keeps commitments (or to be up front if those commitments will not be kept) and accepts responsibility for not only successes but also failures. It is also critical to "tell it like it is," not to bury the bad news.

Build a Foundation with Others

The foundation of influence begins with a close examination of yourself. Also critical to that foundation is a deliberate and purposeful focus on others, as shown in Figure 4.2. That is, you need to be strategic with your influence by taking the time to think about it and positioning yourself to be influential in the future, even though you might not yet know what outcomes you'll be trying to influence.

To understand what we mean by *deliberate* and *purposeful*, it is helpful to think again of being a surfer in the midst of a sea of waves. You watch the waves to learn about how they break, whether the wind is onshore (not good for surfing) or offshore, and how strong it is. You check for any tough currents that must be avoided and for

---

Exhibit 4.3. Measuring a Level of Trust.

Assess how frequently you might behave in ways that could compromise others' trust in you:

Shows arrogance: To what extent might others see you as a bit puffed up with your own importance?

       Never _____   Sometimes _____   Often _____

Promotes personal self-interest: To what extent might others perceive your priority as "What's in it for me?"

       Never _____   Sometimes _____   Often _____

Deceives: To what extent are you perceived to shade the truth?

       Never _____   Sometimes _____   Often _____

Breaches commitments: To what extent might others have doubts about your dependability in meeting commitments and honoring established decision processes?

       Never _____   Sometimes _____   Often _____

Deals unfairly with others: To what extent might others perceive your actions as unfair?

       Never _____   Sometimes _____   Often _____

Shifts blame: To what extent might others perceive you as avoiding personal responsibility for problems or mistakes?

       Never _____   Sometimes _____   Often _____

Diminishes others' dignity: To what extent have your actions (or inaction) conveyed lack of respect for others?

       Never _____   Sometimes _____   Often _____

Harbors envy: To what extent might it seem like you envy others' success?

       Never _____   Sometimes _____   Often _____

Neglects others' development: To what extent is developing others seen as one of your lower priorities?

       Never _____   Sometimes _____   Often _____

Avoids confronting unjust actions: To what extent do others perceive you as a person unwilling to take an unpopular stand on the basis of principle?

       Never _____   Sometimes _____   Often _____

Holds grudges: To what extent do others perceive you as not letting go of hard feelings, and finding ways to get even?

    Never _____   Sometimes _____   Often _____

Avoids effort to help others: To what extent are you seen as a person who does little to help others during times that matter?

    Never _____   Sometimes _____   Often _____

Making Sense of Your Answers

If you selected "often" or "sometimes" to answer any of the items, then you might be behaving in ways that impact perceptions of your credibility and thus your ability to influence others strategically. Spend time thinking about why people might perceive you in these ways. Then spend time considering why you are behaving in ways that lead to these perceptions. Whether or not you agree with the perception is not the point. If the perception exists, it is probably limiting your credibility.

other surfers—where they are, which waves they catch, who has priority for the wave. You assess the amplitude of the wave and what various maneuvers might be possible given these factors. Then you are ready to catch a wave, perhaps starting with a small one to warm up.

For the strategic leader, being deliberate and purposeful means that you need to step back and reflect on your relationships with others and you need to watch and assess the landscape of relationships around the organization. And then it means you use that information and learning when you step in to shape and enhance those relationships. Two areas in particular we would like to focus on with respect to strategic influence are what we like to call "unnatural" relationships and the political landscape.

Engender Unnatural Relationships. As we discussed earlier, credibility is absolutely essential to influence. One way in which leaders can harm their own credibility is by trying to influence without first building the necessary relationships.

We often say that strategic leadership happens in the white space on organizational charts; that is, no matter what the organization's structure, strategic leadership requires the blending of efforts across its various parts. Therefore, relationships that cross organizational boundaries—internal and external—are particularly important. Strategic leaders create opportunities for alliances that do not form naturally because the organization's structure or the work itself militates against them. These leaders reach out to people, not because they need help on some particular task, but because they are looking for possible connections across the organization and beyond.

Building these unnatural alliances is no easy task. It is often inhibited by organizational culture, structure, and measurement and reward systems. For example, the culture may be one of "You stay off my turf—I'll stay off yours," thus limiting cross-unit collaboration. The U.S. military provides one potent example. Consider the difficulty of working on joint projects in the Pentagon. While people within a service (for example, Army or Navy or Air Force or Marines) strongly identify with that service and see issues through the lens of that service, the complex nature of military operations today requires much broader perspectives. These are particularly difficult boundaries to cross, and there is even a pejorative name for people in the Pentagon who develop such a joint perspective: *purple suiters*. The name signifies people who don't strictly adhere to the mind-set of their respective service. Many organizations besides the military offer similar cultural challenges to leaders seeking to span boundaries.

Even if the culture is not antagonistic toward cross-unit collaboration, organizational structure can make working across boundaries difficult. Although structures are supposed to facilitate work (for example, people doing similar work report into the same area), structures can also create distinctions that can have unintended consequences. The task of the strategic leader is to make those distinctions and boundaries permeable.

Finally, the measurement and reward systems in organizations often pit one part of the organization against another part. The internal competition that ensues might certainly provide a focus and be motivating for some, but it does little to engender collaboration. Additionally, systems such as this can deter people from staying focused on the larger success of the organization as a whole.

So what is a strategic leader to do? Managers operate in a world where organizational culture and measures and reward systems are not perfect. Structures have positive benefits (such as coordinating work) that are hard to let go of. Earlier we discussed the need to build trust to exert influence with others in the organization. Breaking down barriers and creating unnatural relationships is another area where building trust between individuals and groups is important.

One way to build that trust is to be more open with information and data than you might naturally be inclined to be. People are often relatively unwilling to be open and honest with others, even though they want others to be open and honest with them. They prefer that others "lay their cards down" first, and then they might choose to share more once they've heard from others.

Vulnerability lies at the heart of that dilemma. Most of us have had the experience of putting our true thoughts, opinions, and feelings out for others to hear only to be burned by our own words. That experience teaches us to clam up and protect ourselves. CCL research and our experience with leaders show, however, that if you can take the risk to be open with others, it creates a climate where others feel freer to share their thoughts and feelings too. And this goes a long way toward creating trust. Exhibit 4.4 gives some suggestions for getting started.

Be Mindful of the Political Landscape. A book on strategic leadership would be remiss if it did not discuss one of the surest realities of organizational life—politics. At its best, politics is often viewed as a necessary evil in organizations. Stanford professor Jeffrey Pfeffer has studied power and politics in organizations, and he defines political behavior as activities to acquire, develop, and use power and other resources to obtain one's preferred outcomes when there

---

Exhibit 4.4. Suggestion for Development: Creating Trust.

If you want others to be open and honest with you but you feel hesitant to do the same, consider doing the following to create a more trusting environment:

- Begin your trust-building efforts outside work—for example, at your church, in a community organization, or in other community service work that you do.

- When you find yourself strongly agreeing with what has been said because it links to personal aspirations or hopes you have, voice that agreement and the reasons why.

- When you find yourself disagreeing with what has been said, tactfully voice that disagreement and your reasons why.

- Rather than waiting to voice your thoughts and opinions until others have had their turn, try a different tactic: be the first or second person to put your cards on the table.

- As you do each of these things, observe others' reactions. Do they tend to share more or less of their own thoughts and feelings? Is the climate or feeling in the meeting more open?

If you have presented your thoughts and feelings in a positive way (even if you disagree with the prevalent view), you'll likely notice that others are more open to saying what is on their mind. Once you have tried this outside work, pick a particular meeting or group of people you work with to try your new skills. Again, observe others' reactions to see the ways in which they are more open with you.

---

is uncertainty or disagreement about choices (Pfeffer, 1981, p. 70). Because politics is an effort in service of obtaining one's preferred outcomes, the exercise of political behavior can be seen as self-serving. But it is important to realize that those preferred outcomes can also be good—they are not necessarily harmful to the organization. It's just that judgments differ about the value of the outcome to the organization, and that's why those with dissenting opinions can interpret the behavior as self-serving.

If strategic goals were always clear, if the information necessary for crafting strategy were always available, if all groups in the organization held the same values, if decision-making processes and accountability were always clear, then there would be less conflict over the strategic direction and how to achieve it. However, these conditions simply do not exist, particularly in organizations that strive to be more inclusive in the strategy-making and strategy-implementation processes. Similarly, because strategies represent both a guide for decision making and action and a plan for where resources should be invested, they are associated with power in the organization. Therefore, shifts in strategy equate to shifts in power, and conflict is sure to be generated by those shifts. The nature of strategic leadership involves bringing about change amid diverse and often contradictory opinions, so uncertainty abounds and the political landscape is a very real element of the strategic leader's life. Hence, politics is one necessary mechanism by which people and groups within organizations can reach agreement on these complex decisions.

But here is the problem. Because politics is a natural part of the strategic leader's life and political behavior can be seen as self-serving, organizational politics can limit the leader's credibility and ability to influence. This conundrum leads to a basic question for strategic leaders: how can they influence others effectively, given the reality of organizational politics, while maintaining their credibility? The developmental exercise in Exhibit 4.5 can help you answer that question.

Some people pride themselves on not being political. They feel strongly that the logic and technical or business merits of their ideas should stand on their own. This can be a naive assumption—just ask someone who has had a great idea for the organization, has done everything possible to influence others, and yet could not convince the organization to adopt the idea. For those who are not used to navigating the political landscape, the exercise described in Exhibit 4.6 can help you get started.

The political landscape when you are attempting to influence upward is often the most challenging and unknown terrain. One element to consider is timing of your influence attempts. Floyd and

---

Exhibit 4.5. Suggestion for Development:
Politics and Credibility.

Here are some ideas to keep in mind about maintaining credibility as you find your way through the political landscape:

- Because political behavior is often viewed negatively—or at best, suspiciously—examine your own motivations with care and honesty. Knowing who you are, why you do what you do, and how your behavior impacts others is critical to ensuring that you are operating with the organization's best interests in mind.

- In communicating to others, speak about long-term issues that are fundamental to the organization and how your ideas help achieve these. Letting people know you are striving for the same outcome as they are will help them to connect to your proposals.

- Recognize that you might not achieve optimal results when the political landscape is difficult, but achieving satisfactory results is better than achieving nothing at all. It also shows that you are willing to give as well as take.

- Keep your endpoint in mind, and be open to other ways to get there. You might have to try several different ways, or only one way that is very different from what you imagined. But usually, that endpoint can be achieved in many ways, so do not get frustrated if your method of achieving it does not survive.

- Over time, show through your results that you are furthering the goals of the organization.

- Be careful about labeling others as political when you perceive them to be acting in self-serving ways. You might not have all the information, so strive to understand how they view their ideas as furthering the organization—not just themselves. In short, model the behavior you would like others to show toward you when they don't fully understand your intentions.

Exhibit 4.6. Suggestion for Development: Understanding the Political Landscape.

The first step in finding your way through the political landscape is to understand it. Consider a particular challenge you are dealing with and trying to influence around. Draw a "political map" to demonstrate who might be connected or aligned around potential solutions to this challenge. Consider all the expected opponents, supporters, and those who might be affected or whose help you might need, even if they might not have a strong opinion. Simply thinking through the various stakeholders in this way can be helpful. Once you have completed your map, go through these steps:

- Look at the map to see who is grouped together. Why are those people aligned? What common goals, perspectives, and beliefs do they share?

- Strengthen your support system by asking those members who are close to you on the map to express support for the idea and give it visibility where possible.

- Generate interest among those who do not have strong opinions by talking about it with them, sharing the data and information you have, inviting their input, and developing contingencies to address the concerns they have.

- Lessen the resistance of those who are opposed by anticipating their arguments and building in compromises or solutions to address those arguments. If possible, talk to them and others to ensure that you fully understand their positions. In communicating to them, work to articulate the advantages they can reap from adopting your position.

- Consider the potential of work assignments. Are there people who are opposed to your ideas that you can assign to various projects or task forces so that they will come to understand the issue differently? Or are there potential key supporters who have not yet been involved enough to understand the issues? Perhaps there is a way to get them involved through various work assignments.

- Find ways to enhance the legitimacy of your arguments by bringing in outside experts. Have these experts work with those who do not have strong opinions or who are opposed to the ideas.

Wooldridge (1996) offer some relevant tips, as shown in the exercise described in Exhibit 4.7.

The political landscape is also an important factor when influencing people outside the organization. Because uncertainty and limited resources also define the interface between the organization and its environment, politics has a role in interactions with these entities. Different strategies exist for managing external politics, and many are similar to those for managing internal politics. For example, one can construct the same kind of political map discussed earlier, but in this case the players on the map would be the various stakeholders internal and external to the organization. In this kind of approach, consider what leverage points are available to the organization. Who can be swayed? If a certain partner were on your side, how might that be to the organization's advantage? The practice of cooperative bidding in the defense industry is an excellent example of managing external politics in this way. In this practice, competitors work together to convince the government that they are the best suppliers of various products and services.

Influence Others by Involving Them in the Process

In Chapter Two, we discuss the importance of involving others in strategic thinking and collaborative sense making. Involving others in that process allows for diverse and important perspectives to be represented so that the overall strategy is better than it would be if it were developed in isolation.

Involving others has another benefit. It helps generate commitment to the final product when others have a say in developing it. The concept of involving others in the process for the purpose of engendering commitment is probably familiar to you. We suspect, though, that when most managers think of involving others as a way of exerting influence, they are thinking of influencing direct reports. Consider how involving peers, bosses, even those outside the organization might be helpful in your strategic influencing efforts.

Exhibit 4.7. Suggestion for Development: Influencing Up.

In *The Strategic Middle Manager*, Floyd and Wooldridge recommend the following suggestions to evaluate whether or not it is a good time to influence (1996, p. 60):

- Consider top management's level of satisfaction with the current strategy. Are they satisfied with progress? If so, they will be less open to new ideas. On the other hand, if they are not satisfied, they may be searching for alternative ideas and will be more open to your perspectives and input.

- Also consider how long the current strategy has been in place. Top managers tend to give new strategies the benefit of the doubt at first, so that they have time to be truly tested. At this point, they will be less open to new ideas, particularly because they have likely endorsed this strategy and will still have some level of enthusiasm for it. "Older" strategies, however, will have had the opportunity to show their limitations. Top managers are typically more open to seeing the flaws and therefore are more willing to consider other options.

Consider the case of Andrew Cole, vice president of human resources for American Power Conversion (APC), a $1.3 billion organization that makes power control devices. Cole learned that the CEO was concerned about lack of bench strength in the company. APC was not in a position to grow through acquisitions because it did not have leaders in place to take over those acquisitions. Despite a long history of success in terms of strategy and implementation, APC executives had paid little attention to leadership development. Cole was tasked with an executive development initiative.

In the early stages of this initiative, Cole realized its complexity. One of his biggest concerns was that he did not want to be seen as the driver of the initiative. He worried that it was risky to have this seen as his project. So his first step was to have the CEO invite several executives (Cole's peers) to join in a pilot program to try out some leadership development experiences. The plan was for the group to assess the program and experience, and to determine what they would need to do to support these efforts internally if they chose to continue down this path. In addition to getting more input on the process, Cole wanted to engage these executives in leadership development activities so that they would feel more committed to those activities. Although he had some ideas about what leadership development should look like in APC, he put those ideas aside in favor of bringing his peers and his boss into the development process.

Cole knew that involving others in the process would help to generate commitment because

- It helps people understand the context, the depth and breadth of the issues involved, and the pros and cons of various solutions. That is, it helps to create a common understanding of the entire picture.
- It helps to develop consensus around the direction chosen so that the group will pull together to make it happen.
- It sends a message that others' input and perspectives are valued—that they add something to the organization beyond getting the work done.

Create a Common Understanding. When people participate in a process, they immediately have access to much more information and develop broader perspectives than they would if they just heard of the final product in a presentation. They hear the pros and cons of different possible solutions; they hear the depth of thinking that others engage in, the questions that are asked and answered, and the level of commitment others have to the organization's goals. They gain an implicit understanding of the situation, the possible paths to take, and why a particular path was chosen. This implicit understanding is vital when it comes to strategy and direction, because executives rely on it to guide their day-to-day activities and they use it to evaluate and engage in conversations with others.

As a case in point, Cole had been in conversations with us about the linkages between APC's leadership development work and other initiatives in the organization. He had not yet, however, discussed those linkages with the CEO. While the CEO was attending CCL's Leadership at the Peak program, he began to see the connections himself. He called Cole immediately afterward and they began discussing it. He had come to a deeper understanding of the leadership strategy by participating in the work itself, as opposed to hearing Cole talk about it. And he was more committed to the breadth of the work when he understood it more fully.

One might even consider the benefits of involving those outside your organization in strategy development and implementation so as to engender their commitment to your ideas. For example, executives frequently use the tactic of running ideas by board members before actually presenting them at a board meeting. This allows the executive to gauge where the board member stands on the issue. Additionally, it allows the opportunity for the board member to have input to the idea before it is finalized.

Create Champions. Another benefit of involving others in the process is that people begin to share the same perspectives, beliefs, and enthusiasm about it. This enthusiasm makes them more likely to support each other and to assist in the influencing process by championing the idea throughout the organization.

In fact, one of Andrew Cole's objectives, beyond simply involving others in the pilot to get their ideas and their own commitment, was also to create champions of the process. He knew that ultimately these executives could be helpful influencing others, if they themselves were committed to the objectives. In fact, he knew his early efforts at involving others and creating champions were successful when he saw executives including their own people in the leadership development efforts.

Demonstrate That Others Are Valued. Most people like to know that they are helpful to the organization beyond simply completing the necessary tasks of the day. It feels good to them to have their thoughts and opinions listened to and acted upon. These feelings of being valued have strategic importance beyond creating a more caring culture. When people know that they are needed, they are more likely to feel compelled to participate in the strategy-making and strategy-implementation processes in ways that go beyond what you can anticipate. They will keep their eyes and ears open for strategically relevant information, and they will exert the effort to bring forward that information to ensure it is considered. They will work harder to solve problems related to strategic issues. They will trust the judgment of others who value them and therefore will be more committed to directions set forth by those leaders. They will exert the effort necessary to implement the strategies and directions of the organization. Exhibit 4.8 is a developmental exercise designed to help you explore this process.

One of the biggest barriers to involving others is that they may come up with something different from what you have intended;

Exhibit 4.8. Suggestion for Development: Validation and Commitment.

Think of the times when you have felt most valued in your organization.

- What was the context at the time (challenge, situation the organization was facing)?
- What did others do to create the climate where you felt valued? Specifically, think of your boss and other senior managers, your peers, and your direct reports.
- What contributions did you make?
- In what ways did others recognize your contributions?
- How would you describe the impact their behavior had on you?

Think about how you are working with others.

- What contributions are they making?
- What would you lose if they were not present?
- How frequently do you tell them this?

they may have ideas and plans that are different from yours. So involving others can feel risky. That is, you might have to let go of your way of doing things in order to include others' ideas. The danger of not letting go of your ideas in favor of others' ideas is that others may feel manipulated. If you ask for their ideas but don't accept them, it's a sure way to show they aren't valued.

Balancing this risk can be difficult, particularly for thoughtful and bright people who are generally good at solving problems (a description of most executives). In Chapter One we discuss the importance of viewing strategy as a learning process and that it involves discovery more than determination. That is a helpful concept to keep in mind when involving others, and many executives find that it helps them when approaching situations where they need to involve others and demonstrate the value others bring to the process. Rather than determining a solution or an answer, they find ways to let the solution emerge through the work. In fact, framing the project as an experiment might be helpful, as we suggest in Exhibit 4.9.

Influence Others by Connecting at an Emotional Level

Strategic direction, alignment, and implementation require tremendous amounts of persistence and effort, demanding commitment from the heart. Earlier in this chapter, we discuss the

---

Exhibit 4.9. Suggestion for Development: Reframe a Project as an Experiment.

Think of an initiative or project that you are about to undertake. Consider viewing it as an experiment, as opposed to a project. In what ways do you think about it differently? What questions or hypotheses can you form about it? What do you want to learn? Now consider the role others will have in your experiment. What information and perspectives might they have that will inform your hypotheses? Why are their views important in the learning process? What will they bring to the experiment that you could not bring yourself? How can you communicate the value that they bring?

importance of engaging your own heart by being clear about your passions. You also need to engage the hearts of others. Certainly, elements we've discussed already (for example, demonstrating others' value by involving them in the process) will help to engage people's hearts. In this section, we explore other ways to generate that commitment:

- Take the time and make the effort to learn what is important to others.
- Connect to the organization's aspirations.
- Use the power of stories, metaphors, and images to enliven your language.

Learn What Is Important to Others. Your logic for taking a particular direction in your organization likely makes sense to you, since it is based on your own assessment of what is important. Realize that your assessment will be different from that of others and that they will be starting from a different base that might invalidate your logic.

For example, while achieving aggressive profitability targets might be one of the most compelling factors for you personally, people in your organization might be more concerned with changes necessitated by that goal and how those changes will affect them personally. Consider, for example, how those changes might impact the distribution of resources in the organization. Perhaps one or more areas will find their budgets cut, possibly in ways that seriously threaten the attainment of their goals. Try the exercise in Exhibit 4.10 to see ways to reach out to others in your organization.

If you are having difficulty putting yourself in others' shoes, you may not know your stakeholders well enough. You'll need to spend some time with them learning about their needs, perspectives, and desires for the organization. The exercise described in Exhibit 4.11 can help you start those conversations.

Once you have put yourself in the shoes of your stakeholders, you'll be in a better position to connect with them. You can frame

Exhibit 4.10. Suggestion for Development: Putting Yourself in Their Shoes.

In considering others' perspectives related to a strategic challenge or initiative you are undertaking, put yourself in the shoes of your stakeholders with these questions:

- Think of yourself as one of your employees. What are your goals? What concerns have you raised in the past? In what areas is the uncertainty harder to tolerate? How will this strategic change impact you on a daily basis? Is there a way to mitigate the downsides of those impacts?
- Now think of yourself as one or more of your peers. What are your goals for your area? What concerns have you raised in the past that might be relevant here? How can you be helpful in achieving this goal?
- Now think of yourself as your boss. What are your goals and aspirations for the organization? How will this change help achieve those goals?
- Now think of yourself as one of your suppliers. What role do you play in the success of the organization? Similarly, what role does the organization play in your success as a supplier?
- Now think of yourself as one of your customers. How will this change make working with the company better? What challenges have you experienced in the relationship? What is important to you, and in what ways will this initiative impact that?

Exhibit 4.11. Suggestion for Development: Conversations for Learning.

Have conversations with your stakeholders so that you can learn more about their needs and explore with them what really matters to them. Use questions like these to encourage these important discussions:

- Why is that important to you?
- Why do you believe this?
- Why do you feel that way?
- If you could design a perfect solution, what would it look like?

your conversations in ways that let them know you've thought about what is important to them, considered how this strategic issue will impact them, and developed ways, where possible, to mitigate the negative effects. You'll also be in a better state to discuss the positive aspects of the future in terms that are important to them. People are generally more willing to go along with the pain of change if they know they will be better off for it.

Connect to the Organization's Aspirations. Thomas J. Watson Sr. once said, "Whenever an individual or a business decides that success has been attained, progress stops" (Watson, n.d.). Having aspirations for a different and better future allows work to have purpose and meaning, as people want to feel that their efforts are making a positive difference.

An important first step in connecting to the organization's aspirations is to have a good understanding of the personal aspirations of others. It's also important to then link those personal aspirations to the aspirations of the organization. A story from Torstar CEO Rob Prichard illustrates this connection. The businesses within Torstar had been separate and independent operating companies that saw their future as distinct from one another. Prichard began to speak of the organization as a whole, as one entity. He communicated the rationale for the operating companies to be together and interdependent in a way they had never thought of before. He also talked about what their collective goals and aspirations should be. In doing this, he created a sense of mission for all the people of Torstar so that they were committed to the entity and its future in ways they hadn't been before.

For some strategic leaders, it is simply a matter of remembering to talk about the organization's aspirations and link them to more specific goals and aspirations of those you are influencing. However, for most strategic leaders, talking about the why requires a bit more preparation. In many cases, it requires thinking more fully about what you are doing in the first place, as in the exercise in Exhibit 4.12. In fact, talking about the why links to the concepts discussed

> **Exhibit 4.12. Suggestion for Development:
> Linking to Organizational Goals.**
>
> Think of a project or initiative you are working on. Consider the
> following questions:
>
> - What is the overall goal of the project or initiative?
> - How does that goal link to the organization's goals? In what ways will
>   the organization be in a better place because of this work?
> - What steps are you taking to achieve the goals?
> - What might people expect to see as a result of this work?
>
> After answering these questions, craft an "elevator speech" that you
> can use again and again with various stakeholders to link the work to the
> broader goals of the organization.

early in this chapter about first determining what is important to
you and what your aspirations are. If you have that understanding,
then this element of influence simply involves communicating that
understanding to the rest of the organization.

Use the Power of Language. Embedded in the section on aspiration
is the notion that aspirational language, in and of itself, can be influential. For example, Disney is well known for its use of ideas and
words to create a culture that touches both people inside the organization and those outside. Employees at the amusement parks, whatever their jobs, are taught to think of themselves as members of a cast
that is putting on a show, and of their jobs as roles in the performance.
Those words and that perspective have strong influencing power.

The executives we work with understand this power of language,
and therefore, many often lament that their strengths lie in a kind of
quiet impact, as opposed to a charisma that draws attention to them
and their ideas. And some are quite turned off by those who are more
charismatic, feeling that there is little substance beneath the style.
No one would suggest that these executives lose their substance in

favor of style. But we do encourage them to consider how they talk about the organization's goals and various strategic initiatives in order to engage others in a substantial way. And there are some simple ways to do this that do not need to threaten a person's core being or style.

For example, how often do you find yourself telling stories to make a point? Stories are powerful because they create images in their hearers' minds. The human brain naturally links information to form stories and images, so using stories is a simple way to harness that power. Images help us make connections we may not typically make between different content elements and therefore can enhance understanding and recall (see Exhibit 4.13). Images and stories also enhance our ability to connect on an emotional level, as they engage the emotion centers of the brain. In all these ways, they are critical to the strategic influencing process. The developmental suggestion in Exhibit 4.14 outlines a simple way to begin to use stories in your language and to see the power that those stories might have.

Finally, we close out this section with some advice from a master storyteller. In an interview with *Harvard Business Review*, Robert McKee, a well-known screenwriting coach, offered executives advice about telling a story ("Storytelling That Moves People," 2003, pp. 51–55). Compelling stories tell of a struggle of a protagonist against one or more antagonists. Stories without struggle do not engender trust because they don't match life's realities. But stories that do tell of a protagonist who struggles and then prevails in the face of those obstacles are dynamic, realistic, and exciting stories. As you craft a story to influence others around a strategic issue, consider the following questions:

- Who is your protagonist? A customer? One or more employees? A supplier? A key strategic partner?
- What does your protagonist want? What is the core need?
- What is keeping your protagonist from achieving that desire—that is, what is the antagonist? Forces within? Doubt

---

Exhibit 4.13. Suggestion for Development: Picture This.

Read the following five sentences and try to form a vivid mental image of each:

- The toothless bathing beauty hardly ever smiled.
- The noisy fan blew the papers off the table.
- The plump chef liked to jump rope.
- The cheerful choirboy sang off-key.
- The small child sat under the lilac bush.

Now read these five other sentences, and evaluate how easy each one is to pronounce:

- The lanky leprechaun wore lavender leotards.
- The skiing trumpeter started a gigantic avalanche.
- The chocolate choo-choo train chugged down the licorice tracks.
- The medieval minstrel strolled along the babbling brook.
- The captured crook liked to do difficult crossword puzzles.

Now, without looking at the actual questions above, answer the following:

1. Who wore lavender leotards?
2. Who hardly ever smiled?
3. Who liked to do difficult crossword puzzles?
4. Who liked to jump rope?
5. Who started a gigantic avalanche?
6. What blew papers off the table?
7. Who strolled along the babbling brook?
8. Who sang off-key?
9. What chugged down the licorice tracks?
10. Who sat under the lilac bush?

Check your answers by looking back at the bulleted lists. Did you do better with the even-numbered questions? It is likely that you did, because you were asked to form a mental picture that corresponded to those items. You were asked to process the odd-numbered questions analytically. Vivid visual imagery engages the brain, and as a result we tend to recall that information better. Using language that creates images can be very powerful as a means of influence.

> ## Exhibit 4.14. Suggestion for Development: Making Stories.
>
> Try this exercise to practice your skills at using vivid language:
>
> - First, list three bullet points or phrases that describe your organization's greatest strengths. Then put that aside.
>
> - Next, tell a story about a time when your organization was at its best. Our bet is that the three bullet points will be reflected in the story, but consider the different impact of the story as opposed to the bullet points on someone you are trying to convince to join your organization.
>
> - To adapt this exercise to a strategic challenge or issue whose outcome you are attempting to influence, try thinking of the future state the organization would achieve if it were to adopt your approach. What characteristics would you see in the organization should that happen? Now craft a story that describes how people will work together, how your customers will view you, how the competition will react, and so on. Consider sharing your story as you talk about your approach.

or fear? Confusion? Tough competition? Organizational culture? Personal conflicts? Social conflicts? Lack of time?

- What is it like for your protagonist to deal with these opposing forces? How would the protagonist decide to act in order to achieve that desire in the face of these antagonistic forces?

- Do you believe the story? Is it neither an exaggeration nor a soft-soaping of the struggle?

Build and Sustain Momentum

Building relationships as a foundation is vital for a particular influence or persuasion attempt to be successful. Similarly important is what you do after you get the yes. Strategic influence is not a one-time event; rather, it is a process that begins with the foundation of understanding yourself and forming relationships with others and continues through to building and sustaining momentum in the midst of strategic change.

Work can get off track in many ways, so a critical element of influence is ensuring that daily pressures do not become distractions to the long-term goals. One can do this by

- Setting appropriate expectations along the way
- Searching out and celebrating successes
- Sending consistent messages

Set Appropriate Expectations. One of the challenges organizations experience with strategic investments is that these investments might not show results right away and this can run counter to people's expectations. We see the impact of this type of situation in the business simulation in DSL. At the start of the simulation, the financial and performance indicators suggest the company is performing adequately; however, investment in factors critical for the company's long-term success has been low. Participants conclude that they need to invest more money and resources in these strategic areas to get the organization back on the growth curve and move it from adequate performance to sustained competitive advantage.

So in the first phase of the simulation, groups tend to make lots of investments. They then get financial and performance indicators back to measure the impact of those investments, and they are often surprised to see that the company is doing no better—in fact, by many measures it is doing worse. When the information is distributed, you can almost hear the participants gulp and start reconsidering their course. They expected to see success after the first year, and the results just do not meet those expectations.

The typical Western organization demands results right away, so executives are conditioned to make quick assessments of the value of various investments and initiatives. If they don't see early success, they are tempted to cut their losses and move forward. However, there are at least two reasons why success might not show itself right away in strategic change. First, these are long-term initiatives. Effectively creating a quality culture and instilling quality in the processes of the organization, for example, have been shown to take three to five years (Hendricks & Singhal, 1997). It is simply unrealistic to expect to see a return on that investment in a one-year time frame.

The second reason that results may not show themselves right away is that when organizations go through significant change, performance drops because the people in the organization are learning new ways of operating. Execution cannot be flawless right away if the change is significant. There will be missteps as people learn and the organization adapts. In fact, one might argue that seeing a drop in performance means the change is progressing exactly as planned.

The danger of this dynamic is that people in the organization often interpret a lack of immediate success as failure and this interpretation is a key threat to building momentum and expanding the stretch of influence. The strategic leader must preempt those interpretations by setting appropriate expectations inside and outside the organization. Exhibit 4.15 provides an exercise in looking backward and forward to interpret results properly.

Search Out and Celebrate the Successes. In the absence of immediate results of strategic change, people may tend to doubt the direction. When that doubt becomes public, it can create a counterforce that is difficult to overcome. One way to deal with this threat is to set appropriate expectations. In addition, strategic leaders must search out, celebrate, and communicate the successes of efforts that are under way. The point is not to stage events and programs but to show tangible evidence that you are on the right path.

One reason that executives don't do this is that they see the successes as expected and therefore simply move on. This dynamic happens frequently in the orienteering simulation we conduct as part of DSL. Teams in the exercise are typically tasked with finding six to ten or more points as laid out in an unfamiliar terrain. Many of these points are quite difficult to find. Some groups spend twenty minutes or more looking before they find a point. (And sometimes they do not find it and decide to move to the next point.) In any case, it is interesting how infrequently teams celebrate when they

---

Exhibit 4.15. Suggestion for Development: The Progress of Performance.

Think back to a strategic initiative you led or worked on in the past. Since hindsight is twenty-twenty, reflect on the progression of performance in that initiative.

- What, if anything, went exactly as planned?
- What missteps occurred?
- How did those missteps impact the key performance measures of your unit and your organization?
- How were the missteps interpreted? In what ways did you and others react to them?
- Could any of the missteps have been anticipated? Why or why not?

Now think about a strategic initiative or challenge you are facing. What do you believe are the prevailing expectations about your key performance measures and how this initiative links to those measures? Think critically about the potential dips that might occur in those performance measures as the organization and people shift their work, their focus, and their mind-sets. The most important part of this exercise is to communicate with others—both inside and outside the organization—to set appropriate expectations about what will happen. Look for every possible opportunity to do so.

---

have succeeded. Instead, their attention is turned to the next point. When we talk about this dynamic after the exercise, the executives will comment that they rarely celebrate successes in their work either. Achieving success, of course, is what they are paid to do. But while these executives believe that success in a strategic initiative simply means all is operating as expected, they are not remembering that others may still be on the fence and so the influence process is not complete. Those on the fence need to see tangible evidence that the initiative is working.

Finally, since strategic change is typically ambiguous, people who are already in agreement with the change may still be unclear as to what they should be doing differently. They are in a learning mode, and your encouraging and reinforcing their actions is an important part of that learning process. They may just need to hear that they are moving in the right direction and are working toward the right outcomes, even if they can't see the whole picture just yet.

Send Consistent Messages. Finally, it's important to consider the extent to which you can influence or even stop other potentially distracting messages from being communicated. If your approach to the strategic issue requires a change in people's behavior, it's a good idea to identify any other organizational systems, processes, or structures that might encourage different behavior from what you want to see. The executives at Neoforma had to pay particular attention to these more systemic issues. Prior to their last strategic change, the company was almost totally focused on the relationship with Novation. For example, one of their key measures was the number of Novation member hospitals that had adopted the technology. As the company moved toward ensuring and promoting success with its installed base, this measure had less significance and, in fact, too much attention to it could have been distracting people from the core need. New measures of performance were created to focus people on the installed base, including, for example, the number of new products adopted by that base of customers.

In *Good to Great*, Jim Collins presents an interesting perspective on where alignment falls in the process of generating momentum. He says, "The good-to-great leaders spent essentially no energy trying to 'create alignment,' 'motivate the troops,' or 'manage change.' Under the right conditions, the problems of commitment, alignment, motivation, and change largely take care of themselves. Alignment principally follows from results and momentum, not the other way around" (2001, p. 187).

In other words, Collins suggests that you focus on generating and demonstrating the step-by-step results, using a process like the one outlined in Exhibit 4.16. That will engender the commitment and momentum and get more people on board with you. They will then help in terms of the alignment piece.

**Exhibit 4.16. Suggestion for Development:
Share the Experience.**

As you begin to see successes with your strategic initiative, gather together those who have been part of those successes to explore their experience of alignment.

- What are the key three to five things they are doing to generate these successes?
- In what ways are the organization's measurement and reward systems, information systems, structure, and other processes facilitating their work?
- Are there ways in which these variables are limiting their work?

The information you gather can be used in many ways. Ideally, you would change anything that is sending inconsistent messages, but that may not be realistic given your level in the organization as well as competing organizational priorities. At a minimum, use this information to set appropriate expectations in others about what is realistic, given these messages. And as you generate more and more success for the organization, use this information to influence upward regarding the impact of the structure, systems, and processes on that success.

Be Open to Influence

As we close out our discussion of strategic influencing, let us leave you with one last thought. It is as important to be open to influence from others as it is to exert influence over others. Strategic leadership is not about who knows best. Rather, it involves ongoing, collaborative learning, and that means strategic leaders must create a climate where they not only exert strategic leadership themselves but also encourage strategic leadership from others. Some executives may have difficulty believing this statement, particularly those who believe that being open to influence is a sign of being weak. If true strategic learning is to take place in the organization, however, executives need to be mindful of the ways in which they define their own strength and competence, and how those definitions impact others.

Here is a story that provides a powerful example in communicating openness to such influence. Torstar sent its top executives through DSL, and Rob Prichard (who at the time was the COO and CEO-designee) was one of the attendees. He found himself in a somewhat odd situation: his role in the business simulation in the program was at one of the lowest levels, without much power attached to his role. For nearly three days, Prichard enacted his role in the simulation constructively if somewhat quietly. During the debriefing, however, he was explicit in expressing the considerable frustration he'd been feeling as a result of not having his input sought out by the simulation company's CEO. Prichard had realized that he could not influence the simulation's CEO if he never had the opportunity. Few things Prichard might have done could have sent a clearer signal about his own desire for people to be engaged with the CEO in strategic discussions. He clearly wanted people to engage with him—and influence him—in the strategy process.

Communicating an openness to influence is important for a superior in interactions with those lower in the organization. This openness has several outcomes, including creating a climate that allows ideas critical for strategic thinking to come forward. It is also vitally important in peer relationships, where the competitive pressures can overwhelm such an approach. In a sense, openness to influence with peers is an outcome—a benefit—of having formed unnatural and trusting relationships. This is particularly important in the context of a strategic leadership team, as we address in the next chapter.

Connecting Influencing to Thinking and Acting

We conclude the two preceding chapters with a discussion of how strategic thinking, acting, and influencing interact. In this chapter, we have focused on strategic influencing. It cannot be isolated from thinking and acting.

For example, the two elements of the foundation of influence are closely related to strategic thinking. Becoming clear about your passions is similar to how organizations become clear about their key drivers. But in this case, the clarity you are seeking is for yourself, not your organization, and you cannot have that kind of clarity for yourself without engaging in some significant strategic thinking. Similarly, being very deliberate about building your foundation with others requires reflection to understand and invest in unnatural relationships, as well as to find your way through the political landscape and keep your credibility intact.

Skill in exercising strategic influence tactics and building momentum for the strategic initiative also requires a combination of reflection and analysis to better understand where, when, and why this skill should be applied. Finally, and perhaps most obviously, the overlap between thinking and influencing is best exemplified when you involve others in the strategic process. That is, in Chapter Two we discuss the importance of involving others in the strategic thinking process to make common sense. Not surprisingly, involving others in the process has influencing benefits too.

There are also many overlaps between acting and influencing. Consider, for example, the work of facilitating coordinated action across the enterprise that we discuss in Chapter Three. One component of this work is to ensure that you are not sending mixed signals. In this chapter, we discuss the importance of sending consistent messages to ensure that your influence attempts are not met with confusion. Similarly, in Chapter Three we discuss the need to create conditions for others' effectiveness by, for example, balancing direction and autonomy. When viewed from the influence perspective, autonomy would not be needed if you did not need others to feel committed and engaged in the work they are doing.

Earlier in this chapter we discuss some of Andrew Cole's efforts to engender commitment to the executive leadership development initiative at APC. Remember that he chose to engage in a pilot process, through which other key leaders were invited to participate in leadership development activities. One purpose was to create buy-in to those efforts (strategic influencing), which he did. But even conceiving of the first step as a pilot represents strategic acting.

Cole knew that leadership development was not optional, but exactly how to carry out that required development was not clear. He took action in the face of uncertainty and then invited people to review the process and make it better for the future. Herein lie elements of strategic thinking: as people engaged in the process, they shaped it and made it better for themselves and for the organization.

This overlap in thinking, acting, and influencing does not happen by chance. In fact, they must complement each other if leaders and organizations are to enact strategy as a learning process. And as you will see in the next chapter, thinking, acting, and influencing also work together within strategic leadership teams.

Chapter Five

Strategic Leadership Teams

While collaboration in making and implementing strategy happens in myriad ways and in a variety of forums, one that demands particular attention is the strategic leadership team (SLT). In our work with executives and organizations, we define these as teams whose work has strategic implications for the organization. Teams that are formally chartered to develop strategy or do strategic planning certainly represent SLTs, but other teams also qualify. Similarly, we are not necessarily referring only to the top team in an organization. Top teams are clearly SLTs (though they don't always function as such), but they are not the only ones.

The Definition and Role of Strategic Leadership Teams

A strategic leadership team is a team whose work has strategic implications for a particular business unit, product line, service area, functional area, division, or company. Just as strategic leadership is different from general leadership (see Chapter One) and strategic influence is different from general influence (see Chapter Four), SLTs are differentiated from other teams in the organization by the work they do. If the work of the team is in service of the long-term success of the organization, then the team is a strategic leadership team.

It might be useful to consider a few examples of SLTs. One example is a team that is tasked with developing the next generation of products in a firm that has innovation as a strategic driver. The work of an SLT might also be linked to the overall strategy and direction of the organization in other, less direct ways. Consider, for example, the top people in a particular functional area of the organization who view their role as ensuring that the function supports the strategy of the organization. Some examples of teams in this category that our DSL program executives have served on include a distribution operations leadership team, a sales management team, and the senior finance staff. A final example is a team that is chartered to design a new process for the organization, such as a continuous-improvement team. Such work has strategic implications because it has impact across different organizational units.

The SLT is a critical element in the strategic leadership process because teams represent the confluence of information in an organization. That is, people come together and bring multiple perspectives, different sets of data and information, and different experiences. In effective teams this breadth of information is blended in ways that can't happen with any single individual. In a sense, teams have the potential to fill the white space on the organizational chart where strategic leadership happens.

SLTs Exist throughout the Organization

An informal poll of readers of CCL's electronic newsletter asked them to tell about the SLTs they serve on (Beatty, 2003). While more than half of the respondents indicated that they were below the senior management level, 97 percent of the respondents indicated that they had served on at least one SLT in the last five years. As our respondents described the type of work their SLTs did, we found that they were engaged in the actual work of the organization: improving processes, running cross-functional initiatives, and supplying leadership at the functional level, to name a few. Based on this informal evidence, we believe that strategic leadership indeed occurs at levels below senior management.

Executives in CCL's Developing the Strategic Leader (DSL) program support the perspective that SLTs exist throughout the organization. Prior to attending DSL, they complete an instrument called the Strategic Team Review and Action Tool (STRAT; see Appendix B). Participants are asked to identify an SLT they serve on—either as the leader or a member. They then answer several dozen questions related to the team's functioning and leadership, as well as members' interactions with each other. Example items include "Members of this strategic leadership team trust and respect each other" and "This strategic leadership team understands the threats and opportunities in the external environment." While the typical DSL participant is at the vice president level or above, we do have director-level participants and occasionally senior managers. Despite the range of participants in our program, they are all able to identify and survey one of their SLTs.

Sometimes SLTs do not function well simply because members do not think of themselves as furthering the sustainable competitive advantage of their organization. This might happen when members get caught up in day-to-day activities and pressures and let their perspectives on the overall value they provide to the organization slip into the background. It's often helpful for these teams to step back and refocus, to gain the big-picture perspective and bring it into the foreground again. Exhibit 5.1 may prove useful in this effort.

The Top Management Team as an SLT

Although SLTs clearly exist throughout the organization, most people think about the top management team as a strategic leadership team. Much has been written about top management teams in organizations. There are debates about whether or not this group really is or should be a team (see, for example, Katzenbach, 1997), whether leadership at the top rests on the shoulders of the CEO, whether the work of the CEO is really shared by that individual and the top team (for example, see Katzenbach, 1998; Nadler, 1996), and the ways in which top teams are different from other teams in organizations (for example, see Katzenbach, 1998; Nadler, 1998). Clearly, the top management team is an interesting entity for researchers

---

**Exhibit 5.1. Suggestion for Development:
The Role of Your SLTs.**

Consider the work you do and the teams you serve on. List the SLTs (there may very well be more than one) that you lead or are a member of. For each SLT:

- What is its mission or charter?
- What value does the team provide to the organization? What would the organization miss if this team suddenly disbanded?
- How does this team help your organization ensure its competitive advantage in the industry?
- How do you know when your team has been successful? How do you measure your success? In what ways do these measures align with your mission or charter?
- In what ways are the members of the team interdependent? Could you and the other team members operate independently and still be successful in the work of the team? If so, how? If not, why not?
- Describe the two or three most important ways this team impacts other organizational units.

Consider asking the other SLT members to answer these questions too and to spend some time discussing everyone's responses so that you have a shared sense of the role each SLT plays in your organization.

---

and practitioners alike. You have probably observed your organization's top team and asked some of the same questions that these researchers have—for example, are the members really a team or just a bunch of individuals who get together to share information? There is no doubt that working as a team at the top of an organization is not an easy thing to do. Katzenbach (1997) offers the following reasons why this is true:

- A meaningful, concrete purpose for a team at the top is difficult to define.
- Tangible performance goals (clear, specific, recurring, and measurable) are hard to articulate.

- The right mix of skills is often absent; instead, members are chosen based on their formal position.
- The time commitment is too high for most busy executives.
- Real teams rely on mutual accountability; executives, however, have excelled by being individually accountable.
- Nonteams fit the power structure; that is, executives are used to a hierarchy that provides clarity about leadership and decision making.
- Nonteams are fast and efficient; executives typically have little patience for the work of energizing and aligning teams.

Despite these difficulties, at least some of the work of the CEO and top management requires teamwork. In fact, Katzenbach (1998) argues that the best CEOs know how to distinguish between work that requires teamwork from the top management group and work that does not. These CEOs are also able to lead the group differently according to the situation.

The question remains whether the strategic leadership responsibilities at the top of the organization are such that the top management group needs to function as a team. And our answer is yes, the top management group should approach this work as an SLT because crafting a strategy for the organization and leading the organization through the learning process requires the interdependence of members at the top of the organization and cannot be done in isolation. Exhibit 5.2 provides some hints on how to be successful in creating a top-level SLT.

When SLTs Fail

Have you ever been part of a team that included talented individuals with resources and commitment but whose performance was less than expected? In some way, when they came together, the members encountered obstacles to their effectiveness beyond any individual's skills and abilities. For example, maybe it was a team

Exhibit 5.2. Suggestion for Development: Creating an SLT at the Top.

Creating a climate where the top management group functions as a strategic leadership team is difficult. The following suggestions (based on Katzenbach, 1997) can be helpful:

- Ensure that the strategy-making work is defined and viewed as a collective work product. That is, emphasize that the team members must apply different skills, perspectives, and experiences to produce the strategy in ways that are not possible by the members working on their own.

- Shift the leadership role. This might be particularly difficult in a top management team, as people clearly look to the CEO as the leader. However, in real teams the leadership is viewed as a process, not a position. That is, it shifts from person to person depending upon who has the knowledge or experience most relevant to the particular issue at hand.

- Build mutual accountability. Executives are used to being held individually accountable. In the true teamwork necessary for strategic leadership, the executives will need to approach this in a different way. Katzenbach offers the following distinguishing phrases to make the point: "We hold one another accountable" as opposed to "The boss holds us accountable" (1997, p. 89).

that consciously or unconsciously adopted a norm of not challenging the leader's opinions. Frequently in these situations, poor decisions result since relevant information and perspectives are not raised. This is one of the many ways in which a team's ability can be less than the sum of the abilities of its individual members.

Although we do not consider athletic teams to be SLTs, they do provide some vivid examples of the whole being more—or less—than the sum of its parts. On one hand, there is the gold medal win by the U.S. Olympic hockey team in 1980. It was an inspiring win because this group of individuals was not supposed to win, given their talents and capabilities; yet combining those individual talents and capabilities into a team created more than anyone expected. Now fast-forward to 1998. By virtually any measure, the U.S. team in 1998 was even better than the 1980 "miracle" team. That's because policies governing team membership had changed by then, and the roster was populated with all-stars from the National Hockey League. Unfortunately, however, the 1998 team did not advance past the quarterfinal round. This "dream team" composed of great individual athletes just wasn't good enough as a team.

Strategic leadership teams are also often composed of individual all-stars, such as successful senior executives and people with considerable technical expertise and experience. In our informal poll, only 40 percent of respondents rated their teams as effective or very effective in meeting their responsibilities (Beatty, 2003). That means that 60 percent of the teams were perceived to be less than effective. Unlike that of a sports team, the ineffectiveness of an SLT reverberates throughout the organization and can have a lasting impact beyond the life of the team. In the most serious situations, ineffective SLTs can threaten the very existence of the organization, impacting people's jobs and lives. At a minimum, when SLTs have difficulties—such as balancing tactics and strategy or communicating throughout the organization—the consequences are likely to be greater than when individuals have these problems. SLTs involve more people and more resources, and they reach deeper, wider, and further into the future of the organization. Their impact is felt more widely than the impact of any individual. That's why it's important for SLTs not to parallel the record of the 1998 U.S. Olympic hockey team—great individual players, but disappointing team performance.

A Case in Point

Here's an example. One CEO we worked with told a story about a team that failed in his organization. The organization had just been through an employee opinion survey, and several issues were identified for further exploration. Cross-functional teams were formed to gather and analyze information and to make recommendations to senior leadership regarding possible actions. Each of these cross-functional teams represented a different SLT, and their success was very important to the company's senior leadership. The senior leadership tried to demonstrate that importance in many ways. Most visibly, a different senior executive championed each of these projects. That role included selecting team members, scheduling and facilitating team meetings, providing information and resources to the team, and coaching the team.

One team's task was to examine benefits provided to employees, since this was a problem area on the opinion survey. The team was populated with middle-tier employees; it did not include junior staff members or senior management (with the exception of the executive champion). It was expected that the team would make recommendations in the interest of the broad employee base and company overall. But that is not what happened.

First, not everyone on the SLT understood that it was a recommending body rather than a decision-making body. Additionally, since the team did not access financial information available to it, it did not evaluate the financial impact of its decisions on the company. Finally, team members emphasized their personal and parochial wants and needs in their deliberations rather than looking at the issue from the perspective of the broader employee population.

The team did come up with eight recommendations, but only two were implemented. What's more, senior management had already identified those two ideas. In the words of the CEO, the other six recommendations were "either absurdly expensive or just totally inconsistent with something that a responsible company would do." The CEO commented that his employee population is very bright—95 percent of them have college degrees, and several have doctorates. Thus the issue was not the intelligence of the individuals on the team. Rather, the team failed to think, act, and influence strategically.

Strategic Thinking, Acting, and Influencing in SLTs

As we emphasize throughout this book, many individuals exercise strategic leadership. It's not just the CEO or members of the top team. It's not just other high-level executives throughout an organization. In fact, it's not just individual leaders who think, act, and influence others strategically. Strategic leadership teams do as well. It might seem strange to say that a team thinks or that a team acts. But in important ways teams do so, and they also exercise strategic influence.

To understand how teams exert the processes of thinking, acting, and influencing, think about a common process in most organizations: performance management. Individual managers can go to various training classes to learn performance management skills, such as goal setting and monitoring, coaching, and recognizing others. Based on training and experience, those individual managers might be very capable managers of their people.

At the same time, the process of performance management can happen within teams too. Suppose, for example, that within a department the individual managers meet as a team to collectively review the performance of their people. A scenario like this would not be surprising: Based on the discussion that takes place, the managers gain a new understanding of their people. In every group, many employees have not been staying up-to-date on new technology, and the managers all come into the meeting believing that their people just need to put more effort into it. During the meeting, however, the managers find themselves talking about the lack of resources available, so that they have too few people and too few dollars for training. Additionally, the reward system within the organization encourages meeting deadlines at all costs. The managers' understanding deepens as they listen to one another. They come to a different understanding of the situation simply because they are tackling the performance issue in a collective way. They even choose to take collective action to resolve the common challenges they experience. In short, the team itself is engaging in performance management.

Think of one of your strategic leadership teams. In what ways does the team think, act, and influence? As a guide to answering those questions, let's look more closely at each of these processes.

SLT Strategic Thinking

When evaluating the extent to which a team is thinking effectively, several different questions should be considered, including these:

- Does the team have access to the strategically relevant information it needs to make decisions?
- Does the team's composition ensure that key strategic perspectives and expertise are present?
- Does the team apply the competency of "making common sense" out of the information available to it?

First, any team must have access to the information it needs to make competent choices. That data must be valid and useful in the process. SLTs in particular must check that they are relying upon measurements and data that are consistent with the drivers of the organization, and not simply data that have always been used for this type of decision. SLTs should also ensure that they have information about the external environment and industry, as well as the internal environment of the organization. Are the measurement and information systems set up to give the team access to these types of information? Does the SLT have norms that encourage taking a strong look at all of these types of information? And finally, does the team actually use that information when it is available?

A classic example of a team that might limit the information coming to it is a top management team that does not have sensors out in the organization to really know what is happening, what the employees believe to be important, and which processes are working and which are not. This team is overlooking important pieces of data that are vital in assessing the health of the organization.

A second question an SLT should consider when examining its thinking ability is whether or not the composition of the team ensures that key strategic perspectives are present. Having appropriate team composition allows for multiple perspectives to emerge and interdependencies to be identified. If critical perspectives are not present, the ensuing conversation cannot be as robust as necessary. The CEO we discussed earlier specifically cited team composition as an issue in that team's failure. The team included people who were senior-level professionals, but they were not in management roles and so did not have the experience necessary to understand issues from an enterprise-wide perspective. As the CEO said, "We made assumptions about this level of employees' ability to think more strategically than they were probably ever trained to think." Given the necessity for strategic and enterprise-wide thinking, he wished the organization had assigned managers and directors to the team.

You can think of team composition in a strict sense (who, specifically, is assigned to this team?), but you can also think of it more creatively. For example, does a team employ or access temporary members, people who are brought in for a short period because their expertise or viewpoint is needed? In examining the extent to which a team has all the necessary information and perspectives available to it, it's important to consider how permeable its boundaries need to be.

In Chapter Two we discuss the importance of making common sense in individuals' strategic thinking; that is, developing a shared understanding of a situation or an integrating concept that clarifies ambiguity. Because common sense inherently involves collaborative work, an SLT is one place to examine this competency in more detail.

The ability of an SLT to engage in making common sense is a function of many things, including the authority dynamics on the team. Ironically, a strong leader can have an adverse impact on the quality of a team's thinking. We recently worked with a CIO and his direct reports, all of whom worked in a global organization. The CIO was energetic, bright, and passionate about his work. He was well respected by his team. However, his energy and enthusiasm were detrimental because people were reluctant to challenge him. SLT members can be reluctant to challenge a leader for other reasons as well; for example, they may have been punished for doing so in the past.

An SLT's ability to make common sense is also dependent upon the team's norms and skills in having open and honest conversations. Most likely you have had this experience: During a team meeting there is a pause in the conversation. You look around and you know that people are not happy, yet no one speaks. The team is limiting its collective thinking by failing to discuss the "undiscussable." There are many potential reasons behind such scenarios. For example, the leader may discourage open conversation by reacting negatively when tough topics are raised. One approach SLTs can take is to adopt norms that encourage open and honest conversation. At the same time, team members need a level of trust that allows them to feel supported when they do take the risk to be honest. Exhibit 5.3 provides an exercise in assessing the SLT thought process.

SLT Strategic Acting

When considering the extent to which a team is acting strategically, consider these questions:

- To what extent does the team have a clear understanding of its latitude of permissible action?
- To what extent does the team make timely decisions?
- To what extent does the team balance short-term and long-term priorities effectively?

**Exhibit 5.3. Suggestion for Development:
Your Team's Strategic Thinking.**

Think about a strategic challenge or decision your SLT recently
faced. Consider possible challenges and decisions that are broad in
scope—that is, they have the potential to have both far-reaching (the
entire organization, for example) and long-term impacts. Evaluate
the extent to which the team effectively practiced strategic thinking
as it dealt with this challenge. Consider questions such as these in
your evaluation:

- What data did you consider? Was this data readily available to the
  team, or did you need to spend more time gathering it?

- To what extent did you balance the convenience of readily available
  data with the need for valid and strategically relevant data?

- Did you consider both internal (about the organization) and external
  (about the industry, customers, competitors, and so forth) data in the
  decision-making process? Was one perspective weighed more heavily
  than the other? Why or why not?

- Looking back on the decision, is there any information that you wish
  had been available to you that was not? What kept you from having
  that information?

- Who participated in the decision-making process? Were all the
  important perspectives present? If not, were members open to
  accessing others who could bring in those perspectives?

- Were all the important perspectives heard in the various
  conversations, or were some voices overly strong or overly
  weak? Why?

- To what extent did the decision-making process encourage open
  and honest discussions?

Now consider a strategic challenge or decision your team is currently
facing. Do any of these questions need attention in order for your SLT to
be more effective in tackling this current challenge?

- To what extent is there a climate for learning within the team?
- To what extent does the team engender strategic action in others?

Let's look first at the extent to which the team has a clear understanding of its latitude of action. You might be surprised to learn how much confusion can exist about this, even within the very top team in an organization. For example, we were working with the executive team of a firm and one area the group felt needed improvement was strategic planning. Among the executives on this team, however, perceptions differed about what, specifically, the issue was. Some members felt that the strategic direction was clear but that they had little built-in accountability to ensure progress in that direction. Others felt that they had not set strategic direction at all but instead were only doing annual planning. As the discussions evolved, deep philosophical differences emerged regarding the role of the executive team in setting strategy: Should they all be involved in it, or should it be reserved for a smaller group of the seniormost executives? The executive team could not make progress on improving the company's strategic planning processes until it had a common understanding of its role in the process. This type of confusion in a strategic leadership team is not uncommon.

Have you ever been part of a team in which, after a couple of meetings (or when things get tough), members look at each other and ask, "Why are we here? What is our task? Do we have control over this issue?" This situation arises when a team is not empowered, when it does not clearly understand what latitude it has for action. This is a critical element in a team's ability to act strategically. SLTs need to know their boundaries, what they can do and what they can't do, in order to act strategically. If they don't have this understanding, they will have difficulty creating strategic clarity for others in the organization.

Even when boundaries are clear, the SLT must also make timely decisions. Is this a team that spends most of its time talking about issues but never charting a course to deal with the issues? In many ways, this area of team functioning is the team corollary to an individual's ability to deal with uncertainty in the decision-making process. Some teams analyze and analyze before coming to some decision. That's an overemphasis on thinking, if you will, that can be detrimental in the long run.

Another area related to strategic acting involves the team's ability to balance and integrate short-term action with long-term action. This ability (or lack thereof) becomes most apparent when something unexpected happens in the organization—for example, the quarter's results are lower than expected. Does the team immediately cut investments that were to have yields in the long term, such as investments in quality or leadership development?

In the chapter on strategic acting we discuss the importance of a learning orientation for individual strategic leaders. The same is true for teams. For teams to act strategically, they must foster a climate of learning in the team itself. That climate can be affected by certain norms—how mistakes are handled, for example. Do members examine the mistakes in a nonjudgmental way for their learning value, or do they jump to apportion (or avoid) blame? Has portraying individual competence become such a dominant norm that there's a spirit of one-upmanship? Is it a risky place to say, "I don't know"?

SLTs should also consider the extent to which they encourage—or discourage—strategic action in others. For example, what impact does the team have on the climate for innovation in the organization? Are there norms within the team regarding how others' failures are handled that reach out to the rest of the organization? For example, if the team is quick to ridicule other parts of the business that have failed, that will send a message to organization members that failure is too risky. Also consider the way in which the team as a whole facilitates coordinated action throughout the organization. Inherent in this aspect of team performance is the need for everyone to be in agreement regarding what that action should be. Exhibit 5.4 provides an exercise designed to explore these points.

**Exhibit 5.4. Suggestion for Development:
Your Team's Strategic Acting.**

Think again about the strategic challenge or decision your SLT recently faced that you reviewed with respect to strategic thinking. For this exercise, evaluate the extent to which the team practiced strategic acting effectively as it dealt with this challenge. Consider questions such as these:

- Did team members understand what the team's task was? Did team members agree regarding what was under the team's control and what was not under its control? If not, what impact did the disagreement have?

- In what ways did the team balance its need for data and information with the need to make a decision? If it leaned toward more information, did the team reach a point where the additional information did not help with making a decision? What, in hindsight, kept the team from making a decision?

- In what ways did the team balance its need for success in the short term with the long-term implications of this strategic challenge? If these needs were not in balance, why weren't they?

- How were mistakes handled within the team? Were members quick to point out what went wrong and who was responsible? Was there a tendency to assign blame or a tendency to learn from mistakes and solve problems?

   Now consider a strategic challenge or decision your team currently faces. Do any of these questions need attention in order for your SLT to be more effective in tackling that challenge?

SLT Strategic Influencing

An effective SLT must engender commitment to its strategies, goals, and objectives among its own members as well as throughout the rest of the organization. With special regard to the latter, the team needs to speak with one voice to the rest of the organization. This is not an easy task. Four critical strategic leadership team competencies go into this process:

- Effective influence between the team members
- A foundation of relationships with other key teams in the organization
- Consistent influence throughout the rest of the organization
- Openness to influence from others

SLTs should first examine the influence processes within the team. Who are the most influential members on the team and why? Are the power differentials so great, for example, that only some points of view will be attended to—regardless of their merit? Do team members trust each other? If they don't, then mutual influence and effective collaboration become quite difficult.

Without a foundation of mutual trust, efforts to shape each other's thinking will have marginal impact. The team will then be far less likely to make common sense effectively or to collectively embrace bold strategic decisions with the levels of commitment essential to championing them throughout the organization. Because SLT members often come from different parts of the organization, they have relatively little interpersonal experience together and are also likely to run into apparently competing departmental interests and priorities.

Trust and strong relationships must also exist between the team and other key teams in the organization. It's important to identify, for example, those ways in which the work of one SLT is interdependent with that of other SLTs. Do these teams understand each other's goals and roles? Do they understand the constraints each faces? Do they understand their potential points of overlapping responsibility or authority? Do they know how the success of the organization is dependent upon its teams collaborating effectively?

A third area for consideration is the extent to which the team sends consistent signals throughout the organization. How often have you believed that one thing was decided in a meeting, only to hear later that other team members are talking about it in different ways? These are not necessarily deliberate acts; people may not be purposefully spinning the decision in ways that work for them (although that happens too). Often participants have innocent but meaningful differences in understanding that—as messages spread through an organization—confuse others about actual strategic direction and priorities. Here, too, the issue is even more important for SLTs than for other teams. That's because people across the entire organization will understand and interpret communications from the perspective of their own primary group (for example, manufacturing, marketing, or sales).

This type of situation is common in the simulation used in the DSL program. Say, for example, that three executives from the headquarters staff agree to disseminate the decision that Hawley-Garcia (the fictional company featured in the simulation) will become a global company. Sometimes they even announce this in front of the entire group of Hawley-Garcia's corporate officers. Sounds simple, right? When the headquarters executives then visit separate regional meetings, however, those regional executives often ask for clarification. It's interesting to see—once you go beyond "sound bite" descriptions of decisions (for example, becoming a global company)—how radically different interpretations of a decision can come from people on the same headquarters team, people who have presumably reached a common decision. For example, being a global company could mean anything from "Be aware of what is happening in other regions, but it doesn't really impact your own decisions" to "You should be talking to the other regions and making these decisions in common, because we don't want to duplicate efforts throughout the organization."

Finally, it may be as important for an SLT to be open to influence from others as it is to be influential itself. We have discussed how important it is for individual leaders to be open to influence, and this is critical at the team level too. This can help improve the quality of thinking, decisions, and buy-in within an SLT, and it can do the same with regard to the reactions of individuals and teams outside the SLT. So members should pay particular attention to the norms in their SLT regarding their openness to information and perspectives from the outside. Exhibit 5.5 provides an

---

Exhibit 5.5. Suggestion for Development: Your Team's Strategic Influencing.

Think again about the strategic challenge or decision your SLT recently faced that you reviewed with respect to strategic thinking and acting. This time, evaluate the extent to which the team effectively practiced strategic influencing as it dealt with this challenge. Consider such questions as these:

- How was influence exerted within the team? Did all members feel they had the opportunity to exert influence? If not, why not? Were all team members committed to the outcome of the decision, or did some just go along?

- In tackling this strategic challenge, did the team require the collaboration of other groups and teams across the organization? If so, what was the relationship of your team with those teams? Was collaboration easy to attain? If there is strain in those relationships, why is that so?

- How did team members present the decision or outcome to the rest of the organization? Was there a consistent message? Did some parts of the organization hear one message and other parts of the organization hear a different message? If so, what was the impact?

- As data and perspectives from others came to the attention of the team, how open were members to this information and influence? Did the team seek to involve others in the process, both to gain new insight and to engender commitment from others in the final outcome?

Now consider a strategic challenge or decision your team is currently facing. Do any of these questions need attention in order for your SLT to be more effective in tackling that challenge?

---

exercise to explore the ramifications of strategic influence at the team level.

Strategic Leadership Teams and the Learning Process

In Chapter One we introduce the notion that strategy is a learning process, and we depict that process as shown once again in Figure 5.1. Through this iterative process of hypothesis testing, strategic

Figure 5.1. Strategy as a Learning Process: Recap.

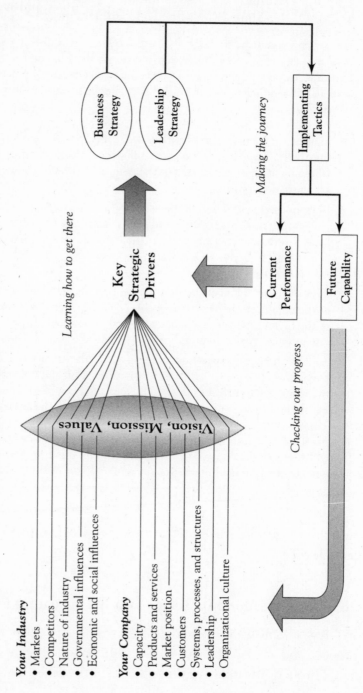

Assessing where we are

Understanding who we are and where we want to go

Your Industry
- Markets
- Competitors
- Nature of industry
- Governmental influences
- Economic and social influences

Your Company
- Capacity
- Products and services
- Market position
- Customers
- Systems, processes, and structures
- Leadership
- Organizational culture

Vision, Mission, Values

Key Strategic Drivers

Learning how to get there

Business Strategy

Leadership Strategy

Implementing Tactics

Current Performance

Future Capability

Making the journey

Checking our progress

leaders gain clarity about the most important success factors in their industry—the drivers—and enact business and leadership strategies to excel at those drivers.

Effective individual strategic leaders use thinking, acting, and influencing to make strategy a learning process in their organizations. Effective SLTs do the same thing to create the climate and the processes necessary for strategy to be a learning process in the organization. Let's examine the elements of the learning process in a bit more detail to see how they apply to SLTs.

Depending upon their level in the organization, SLTs might engage differently in the work of *assessing where we are*. Certainly, top management teams must be attuned both to what is happening in the industry and external environment and to what is happening in the organization. Team meetings might consist of reviews of industry data, internal surveys and performance indicators, and so on. At lower levels in the organization, strategic leadership teams need to be aware of the critical competitive factors impacting their specific work. In addition, it is often these SLTs that have firsthand knowledge of what is happening not only inside the organization but outside it as well. At a minimum, therefore, they have a role to play in communicating those insights upward.

Understanding who we are and where we want to go will also mean different things to SLTs depending on their level in the organization. Clearly, it's important for any team to have a common understanding of the overall organization's aspirations and embrace them. Additionally, SLTs must work to ensure that their own team charter or mission is in support of the organization's aspirations. When the SLT includes diverse members from across the organization, having a shared sense of the future can be more difficult to achieve.

As SLTs gain clarity about their role and the key tasks before them, they should determine areas of focus and priority (strategic drivers) and then set forth on a path to best leverage those drivers and achieve strategic objectives. This is the *learning how to get there* phase of the learning process. SLTs at all levels do set forth strategies, whether or not they call them strategies. Since *strategy* refers to the patterns of choices an organization makes to achieve sustainable competitive advantage, one can look for those patterns to determine the strategy of the SLT. Similarly, SLTs do set a leadership tone for the organization, and this is what we are referring to when we discuss leadership strategy.

Strategic leadership teams are *making the journey* through the operational plans they set and enact. This is perhaps the most familiar place in the cycle for many SLTs, as it reflects the day-to-day tasks and projects that members are engaged in. Placing this work in the context of a learning process will help the team ensure that these projects and tasks are reflected in the strategy of the team and the organization.

Teams are also familiar with the elements of the process associated with *checking our progress*. Measures are not new to most teams. Conversations within the team often revolve around measures because they are a relatively simple way to gauge progress and success. How is a project progressing? Are we going to meet our deadlines? Are we going to meet our numbers for this quarter? How is our customer satisfaction index this month? The most critical element for an SLT, however, is to ensure that it has robust measures that accurately reflect the most critical elements of success for the team, as opposed to measures that reflect what has always been or that satisfy only what the team is able to measure with any level of accuracy.

Finally, teams must reassess where they are strategically. What has changed in the competitive environment that impacts the broader organization? What has changed in the broader organization that impacts the SLT?

Throughout this discussion, it is not our intent to imply that an SLT goes through this learning cycle in isolation; rather, members access other people and teams inside and outside the organization to bring in different perspectives and data, and to move in the direction the SLT has set forth. In short, an SLT is a team with some responsibility to help lead the organization through the cycle. The learning process simply provides a helpful framework for thinking about the team's different leadership tasks.

How the Harlequin Leadership Team Made Strategy a Learning Process

It might be helpful to see how one particular SLT approached strategy as a learning process. Continuing the earlier discussion of Harlequin, we use its leadership team as our example.

Assessing Where We Are

In 2001, Harlequin was in a strong and enviable position. It was the world's leading publisher of romance fiction and controlled the majority of the North American market. It had enjoyed twenty years of profitable growth. But the leadership team was not satisfied with the status quo. After all, the majority of the market in women's romance fiction represents only a small portion of *all* women's fiction. While only modest sales growth was expected in its basic niche, opportunity for growth in the broader market was significant.

Understanding Who We Are and Where We Want to Go

Shortly after taking over as Harlequin's CEO, Donna Hayes refocused the company on its core expertise and identity—a book-publishing company (it had diversified in several ways). She also challenged the members of the leadership team to set significantly higher targets in their respective business areas, their record of solid performance year after year notwithstanding. Finally, Hayes challenged the identity of the team itself. Specifically, she redesignated it the Harlequin leadership team (formerly the Harlequin management committee). More than just a name change, the new label symbolized how the whole team (and not just the CEO) now would be responsible for leading Harlequin.

Learning How to Get There

Shortly after taking over, Hayes held a two-day retreat for the Harlequin leadership team. As part of that retreat, the team identified key drivers in the publishing industry and metrics for evaluating progress and success. Their work reflects what we mean by "systems thinking" and "making common sense."

Hayes and the Harlequin leadership team also took steps to assure that their deeper strategic understanding and philosophy of leadership cascaded throughout the organization. In new all-employee meetings Hayes and Harlequin's CFO and HR vice president clarified Harlequin's strategy for everyone in the organization. Formal leadership development opportunities were provided for the first time to levels below the executive.

Making the Journey

For the next year, each of Harlequin's businesses focused its efforts on its respective strategic drivers. Each monthly business group meeting was organized to highlight current efforts and progress with regard to these drivers. Attention was focused on the extent to which business tactics were consistent with the strategy and these key drivers.

Checking Our Progress

By virtually all measures the following year was a very successful one for Harlequin. Its earnings were much higher than during the previous year. It placed four books on the *New York Times* best-seller list at the same time—a first for Harlequin and a notable achievement for any publishing company. A key factor in this success was enhanced strategic thinking, acting, and influencing in the Harlequin leadership team itself. For example, members engaged more collectively on substantive issues than before, the team was more open to ideas from anyone on the team, strategic priorities were clearer in the team and throughout the company, and there was a higher level of energy on the team. After one year the team had achieved virtually across-the-board improvement on items measuring strategic team effectiveness.

One year after its first strategic retreat with Hayes as CEO, the team met to review its progress. As noted, the year had been a successful one by all measures. But it also was a year of continuing reflection on the industry and Harlequin's place in it. It was during this year, in fact, that Harlequin's new vision (mentioned in Chapter Two) became crystallized: *world domination of women's fiction*. In the context of the competitive analysis of a year before, the rationale underlying that new vision was becoming clearer. The expansion of its market to the broader field of all women's fiction offered growth opportunities otherwise unavailable.

That vision represents a bold destination (*where we want to go*), but it also represents a radical redefinition of company identity (*who we are*). In effect, this represents a change from being a very big fish in a relatively small pond to becoming a big fish in a much bigger and different pond (somewhat different organizational competencies and key strategic drivers likely apply in different genres of women's fiction). To succeed, Harlequin's leadership team knew that it needed to make strategy a learning process and continue strategic thinking, acting, and influencing.

Developing Your Own Strategic Leadership Team

To close out this chapter, we would like to turn your attention to several tools to help you develop your own SLT. These tools are based on the STRAT instrument mentioned earlier in this chapter and provided in Appendix B. STRAT allows SLT members to rate the team on several diverse aspects of the team's overall strategic effectiveness. The purpose of STRAT is to generate conversation within the team about the team's effectiveness.

Appendix C shows a mapping of the STRAT items to the strategy-as-a-learning-process framework. We find this mapping helpful because it provides some organization to the twenty-seven different STRAT items. Additionally, this mapping allows one to look for similarities between some of the items within each element of the process that could be helpful to the SLT. For example, it is possible that an SLT's strengths fall generally into one category. It's also possible that an SLT's weaknesses fall generally into another category. Knowing this can help SLT members focus on what is happening with the team and help the team to improve its performance during the action-planning process.

In Appendix D, we provide specific tips for using the STRAT instrument with your team.

Finally, Appendix E provides comparison data for the STRAT items. Specifically, we've collected data on how nearly 5,300 different managers and executives rate their respective SLTs on the STRAT items. The item averages and standard deviations based on this data are shown in this appendix.

We invite you to use these tools with your SLTs to assess and improve their strategic effectiveness. We believe you will find—as we have—that nearly every SLT has at least one or two things it can do differently to be even more strategic. We also believe you will find—as we have—that because SLTs are embedded in the organization's context, there are certain organization-level variables (for example, culture, structure, systems) that impact these teams. The next chapter will help you better understand the influence of those variables so that you and your team can be more strategic within their context.

Chapter Six

Making Strategy a Learning Process in Your Organization

Up to now we've been focusing on the skills and perspectives individual leaders and leadership teams need to be effective strategic leaders. In this chapter we turn our attention to the broader organizational context in which individuals and teams exercise strategic leadership and the part leaders can play in fostering conditions most likely to encourage it.

Organizational Conditions That Support Strategy as a Learning Process

No behavior occurs in a vacuum. Individuals and teams always exercise leadership in particular organizational settings that can vary dramatically in the way they encourage the strategic leadership we've been describing. The extent to which conditions facilitate or inhibit strategy as a learning process stems from the combined effect of an organization's culture, structure, and systems.

In this section we look briefly at the general nature of these foundational conditions of strategic leadership and at two organizations that differ in their readiness to make strategy a learning process. Finally, we look at specific conditions of culture, structure, and systems that support strategy as a learning process.

The Underlying Conditions: Culture, Structure, and Systems

Organizational culture refers to the taken-for-granted values, underlying assumptions, and collective memories in an organization. Culture represents "how things are around here." It conveys a sense of identity to people in the organization and provides unwritten (and often unspoken) guidelines for how to get along. Military organizations, for example, have cultures different from those of college faculties, and the culture of an investment firm is different from the culture of a research-and-development firm or a freight-hauling company.

Organizational structure is typically depicted as a chart that clarifies formal authority relationships and patterns of communication within an organization. Most people take structure for granted and fail to realize that it's just a tool for getting things done. Structure is not an end in itself, and different structures might exist for organizations performing similar work, each structure having distinctive advantages and disadvantages.

It is generally accepted that structure should serve strategy, not vice versa. How can you be sure, however, that this is the case in your organization? In one interesting example, we have been working with the top team at a $1.3 billion high-tech company that over its history has studiously avoided publishing any organizational chart. A big reason for this is the belief, held by many of its senior executives, that organizational charts by their very nature curtail creativity and initiative. As the company has grown larger, however, increasing numbers of people inside and outside the organization have begun to call for greater clarity about roles and responsibilities—for example, how do you know whom to go to? Who's in charge? The lack of structure creates confusion, uncertainty, and conflict. Yet the senior team still wonders about the answer to a basic question: have we been successful because we've avoided creating organizational charts, or in spite of it?

As with structure, organizational systems ought also to be designed to serve strategy. Four kinds of systems are common to virtually all organizations: *reward systems* (formal and informal practices that determine who and what gets rewarded); *control systems* (policies, procedures, and authorities for decision making, resource allocation, and other organizational commitments); *communication systems* (channels and processes through which goals and plans, information about individual and organizational development, and progress toward strategic objectives are communicated); and *learning systems* (how resources are designed, acquired, evaluated, and distributed for both individual and organizational development).

Case 1: Encouraging University Department Heads to Be Strategic.

A small group of us had been invited by the dean of the College of Liberal Arts at a major university to facilitate a strategic planning process for the college. It was to have taken place primarily in two large meetings of key faculty leaders (for example, department heads, senior faculty, staff agency heads) a month or two apart. The first meeting was to review the report of a needs assessment we had done for the college (based on either phone interviews or e-mail surveys of participants in the strategic planning retreats), to allow participants to share individual visions of their views of an ideal state for the college in the future, and to develop a draft vision statement for the college (using the dean's preliminary draft as a starting point). The second session, planned to be a three-day event, was to make refinements to the vision statement, and from it to identify specific objectives, action steps, and accountabilities to achieve that vision.

The needs assessment we carried out asked faculty members what they perceived to be the primary strengths, weaknesses, opportunities, and threats facing the college. It also asked them on a more personal note what would make these strategic planning retreats worthwhile for them. Their responses reflected a desire to act with greater strategic purpose and champion strategic change for the college; some also reflected a desire to develop greater strategic insight. Here are a few representative comments:

"I would want to feel like everybody's on the same team and that we have identified some realistic next steps."

"I hope we come away with a stronger sense of community."

"I hope we'll be able to get beyond pettiness and our own disciplines."

"It's getting harder and harder to find faculty who will take on leadership roles; I hope we can do things that will turn that around."

Our assessment from the data we'd collected was that participants were approaching the retreats with a general sense of hopefulness, tempered by their personal history with faculty politics and earlier unsuccessful retreats. Another positive sign was the widespread respect for the dean who'd commissioned this process and for the progressive change that he championed.

However, the reception we actually received was quite different from what we had expected. Our interactions with the group felt contentious from the start—so much so, in fact, that the second session never occurred. It was obvious on the first day that this would not be a constructive working relationship. Both sides decided then and there to discontinue the work.

We were stunned, frustrated, and angry. While we accepted our fair share of responsibility for the failure, we were still confused by the seeming disconnect between the hopefulness we'd sensed during the needs assessment and the hostility toward us that was obvious in the meeting itself.

In retrospect, many things contributed to the predicament. Among them was a general antagonistic undercurrent toward business or business methods. The idea of adopting a businesslike strategic planning process at a college was anathema to some. Additionally and perhaps most important, we had completely misjudged the impact of faculty politics on the tone and ultimate outcome of the meeting. Several powerful faculty leaders who had not joined in the needs assessment played pivotal roles in creating an adversarial climate. Hidden agendas were rampant, and the meeting became a no-man's-land for those who'd approached the day guardedly optimistic about participating in a significant institutional change process.

Finally, we realized belatedly that not only was there no shared vision for the college (that was to be part of our task) but there was not even shared understanding of what the college's mission was or should be. In essence, some saw the college as essentially a "holding company" of independent academic departments, while others believed it should be more than the sum of its parts, a force for synergy among the departments and thereby a stronger advocate for itself in the broader university environment.

This experience reminded us once again of the profound way that underlying organizational conditions can either facilitate or obstruct the efforts of individual leaders to think strategically, act strategically, and influence others strategically. In the college, for example, dominant aspects of culture included resistance to change and higher valuation given to academic departments than to the college itself. And paradoxically, while most of the retreat participants seemed perplexed by the challenge of attracting more faculty to leadership positions, the group nonetheless collectively perpetuated some of the very conditions that make academic leadership unattractive and made their task even more difficult.

Case 2: *Catholic Healthcare Partners*. We have already introduced Catholic Healthcare Partners as one of the largest nonprofit hospital systems in the United States. A major challenge for the organization is balancing its mission of being a faith-based healing ministry with the dynamic and evolving challenges of the health care business in the twenty-first century.

CHP's Aspirations. Originally founded by Catholic Sisters, CHP is moving toward primarily lay leadership. Even so, it remains committed to the faith-based values and perspectives on which it was founded, including its mission to provide health care to the poor and underserved.

It is no small challenge for any health care system to provide clinically superior services and remain financially viable; it's even more of a challenge when its mission calls it to serve the poor in the inner city. In a sense, however, that's only half of CHP's challenge. "It requires more than that," says CHP Senior Vice President

Jon Abeles. "It also means living out the values of our organization in the context of everything we do."

An important part of CHP's leadership strategy, therefore, is to make sure those values are understood and embraced throughout the system. "With no more Sisters present in key administrative positions," Abeles says, "it's incumbent upon the leadership team to be able to articulate who we are and what we do in comparison to other health care organizations so that we are aligned with our mission and live our values every day. Leaders in CHP need to have a passion for the ministry and be able to articulate it continuously to our associates and project it in the communities we serve."

Toward that end, CHP has developed a deliberate enculturation process for new leaders in the system. Those leaders might not be Catholic and might never have worked in a faith-based health care system before. Nonetheless, they need to understand and embody those values, and be able to teach them to others.

Leadership Development at CHP. A significant element of CHP's strategy is its approach to leadership development. Leadership development is something everyone at CHP is involved in, from the CEO down. For example, every member of CHP's executive management team works with an individual coach. What's more, the team works with a coach to continually improve its collective effectiveness.

CHP's vision of leadership development for its next generation of leaders came to be known as the leadership academy. Key objectives for the academy included identifying a pool of high-potential executives for higher positions and helping them develop skills in critical leadership areas, building a cadre of next-generation leaders committed to carrying on the organization's mission and values, and imbuing a sense of "system-ness" in executives across the different regions of the organization.

A key component in planning for the leadership academy was to align the organization's strategic priorities with the critical leadership factors that would be needed to meet them. A cornerstone of the leadership development process was identifying the critical qualities CHP leaders would need to possess in the future. Senior leaders met for several days to debate these qualities, eventually identifying five as most critical: a passion for CHP's mission and values, servant leadership, the ability to handle complex mental processes, a bias for action, and the ability to develop others.

The leadership development process that took shape over the next few years was one of unusual depth: multiple classroom sessions focusing on assessment and development of individual and organizational leadership capacity; rounds of action-learning projects based on complex, strategic-level business problems; individual and team coaching; and an extensive evaluation process to track participants' progress, their influence on the organization in the future, and the role of the organization in supporting development and transfer of learning and action.

From the very start, the leadership academy enjoyed strong support and participation from CHP's executive management team, which demonstrated its support for the academy in many tangible ways:

- Identifying, screening, and recommending high-potential individuals for inclusion
- Authorizing the absence of participants from their regular work obligations for the purpose of academy commitments
- Proposing business dilemmas for potential action-learning projects
- Sponsoring, facilitating, and responding to the work of the action-learning teams

CHP has reaped many benefits from its leadership academy, including greater effectiveness of academy alumni as individual leaders, their deeper connection and commitment to the organization's mission and values, and strengthened cross-regional and cross-functional networks among alumni. Other outcomes transcended benefits to individual participants, including action-learning projects that provided greater organizational clarity about partnerships with other health care facilities, reduction in turnover rates of nurses, and a more comprehensive focus on diversity in the workplace.

How Culture, Structure, and Systems Affect Strategic Leadership

The cultures at the college and the health care organization represent quite a contrast. At the college, for example, the power of "how things are around here" became quite clear when we attempted the strategic planning work. The dominant mind-set seemed to be "The college exists so that individual departments and professors can do their work" rather than "Professors and departments work in service of the college and university objectives." It was a culture resistant to systematic change despite the dean's initiatives toward this end.

In contrast, CHP executives conveyed a sense of commitment to the organizational mission in addition to their pragmatic determination to deliver both high-quality service and business results for the larger organization. Most CHP executives displayed a genuine and selfless subordination to a higher organizational cause.

It felt noticeably different visiting the two organizations—at least to outsiders who were there to take part in an organizational intervention (we were not "neutral" visitors). In one organization it felt as if the staff had circled the wagons; in the other we felt like welcome helpers.

We saw notable contrasts in their structures and systems as well. At the college the different departments had little in the way of strategic synergy with each other; the college mostly served as an administrative umbrella providing resources for relatively independent departmental functioning. The impact of systems at the college reinforced this departmental structure.

Take the tenure system as an example. Tenure—a prized status in the academic world—is largely achieved by productivity in independent knowledge work. Reward and recognition systems encourage individual achievement (for example, doing good research, bringing in grants, teaching well). At CHP, on the other hand, the system offers relatively greater incentives to encourage collaborative work within clinical teams, across departments, across hospitals, and so on.

In sum, what we saw at the college and at CHP are organizations characterized not only by two different missions and kinds of work but also by differentially favorable conditions for enacting strategic leadership. In CHP, the combined impact of culture, systems, and structure created fertile soil for making strategy a learning process. By contrast, the culture, systems, and structure in the college seemed to stifle the learning process.

These are just two organizations, each likely very different from your own. Rather than look further at these specific cases, therefore, let us turn our attention toward general aspects of culture, structure, and systems that support strategic leadership.

What Culture, Structure, and Systems Are Best?

That's a bit of a trick question. There is no culture, structure, or system that is *best* in any absolute sense. Some kinds of organizational culture are better suited for dealing with certain combinations of competitive conditions and goals than others; decisions about structure and systems almost always mean trade-offs between advantages and disadvantages. There's no best-for-all-purposes culture, or structure, or system.

But we're not talking about best for *all* purposes here. We're interested in the more specific challenge of creating optimal organizational conditions for strategic leadership as we've described it. What dimensions of culture, structure, and systems best support making strategy a learning process? What do these more hospitable conditions look like? Let's look at specific examples of culture, structure, and systems in which strategic leadership can flourish and in which strategy can become a learning process.

Organizational Culture. This section lists two contrasting manifestations of culture, one that helps participants maintain balance riding the turbulent waves of strategic leadership, and another that doesn't. These represent two quite different environments to work and lead in. As you review them, think about which set comes closer to describing your own organizational culture.

Illustrative signs of a culture that supports strategic leadership and strategy as a learning process:

- People are conscientious about keeping others—even from different functional areas—informed about developments and new initiatives in their areas of responsibility.
- The feasibility and desirability of new opportunities are assessed in terms of the organization's vision, mission, and strategy.
- People talk about the positive example of a task force leader who asked people from diverse parts of the organization to join in solving a major problem.
- People talk about the initiative shown by a manager who saw an opportunity, found the resources to test it, and demonstrated its market viability.
- People generally understand that one of the company's most successful new ventures was originally the idea of someone relatively low in the organization.
- The seeds of new ideas sometimes come from functional areas other than the ones they're ultimately implemented in.
- People know the organization's vision, mission, core values, and strategy, and can apply them to unique or emergent situations.
- There are mementos in offices recognizing cross-functional team achievements.
- You frequently hear things like "try it," "faster," "collaboration," "vision," "cutting edge," and "initiative."

- People celebrate mistakes because the organization learns something valuable from them.
- In both ad hoc work groups and formal teams, authority shifts among members to match the demands of the situation.
- Conversations about strategy occur in both top-down and bottom-up directions.
- The boxes and lines on the organizational chart are thought of as permeable boundaries rather than walls.
- Learning about aspects of the company beyond one's functional group is encouraged and supported.
- Managers have a broad network of organizational relationships extending beyond their routine work groups.
- People readily seek and offer help to others inside and outside their primary work groups.
- There's a sense of energy and excitement about working in the organization; if there's a problem, people feel they can solve it.
- There's a shared sense that *everyone* has some role in the leadership of the organization.
- There is an emphasis upon learning, and an acceptance that part of learning involves sometimes making mistakes.

Illustrative signs of a culture that constrains strategic leadership and strategy as a learning process:

- The desirability or feasibility of a new opportunity is assessed in terms of its conformance to existing policy and procedures.
- Senior executives praise the thoroughness of documentation of department status reports.
- People talk about "that good idea that got away" because it didn't seem to fall clearly in anyone's particular area of authority or responsibility.

- Someone is rumored to have missed a promotion after championing an idea that didn't work out.
- Mementos in offices exclusively recognize individual accomplishments.
- You frequently hear things like "follow procedures," "document carefully," "be efficient."
- The most frequent kind of positive feedback people receive is for managing costs well.
- There is relatively little interaction among people outside their primary work groups.
- It's a common practice to set modest targets that you know you can meet rather than ambitious targets that you might fall short of.
- It often seems as though the right hand doesn't know what the left hand in the organization is doing.
- The chain of command is scrupulously followed.
- People who are effective in self-promotion tend to get promoted.
- The organizational metrics that get the most attention are short-term and functionally narrow.
- People put a lot of effort into making their own groups look good.
- Communication about the organization's strategy tends not to come at all, or only in a top-down and rather cursory manner.
- The degree of competition between peers makes significant cooperation and collaboration difficult, superficial, and infrequent.
- It often feels as if groups throughout the organization have circled their wagons.
- Few people seem to have a sense of how their own work fits into the big picture.

- A sense of powerlessness permeates the organization; if there's a problem, people look for their bosses to fix it.

- Leadership is viewed as the prerogative of select individuals in senior positions of responsibility.

- There is such an emphasis upon individual competence that people avoid situations where they might appear to make a mistake.

Organizational Structure and Systems.   This section illustrates aspects of organizational structure and systems that are likely to encourage strategy as a learning process. In this case, however, we're only addressing the positive side of the equation.

- Managers at all levels have conversations (they don't just hold briefings or pass out documents) about the organization's vision, mission, and strategy, and the implications of those ideas for each group's work.

- Senior managers hold regular meetings with individuals from different levels across different units to discuss current issues in the understanding and implementation of business strategy.

- The organization's most creative people serve on task forces to identify new business opportunities.

- The organization scrutinizes its own processes to identify and remedy barriers to creativity, recognizing a variety of potential causes and solutions.

- Systems and accountabilities exist for scanning the environment broadly to keep abreast of trends in other fields and for disseminating the results throughout the organization.

- Systems exist to measure and reward team and unit performance, not just individual performance.

- Information systems make it easy for ad hoc groups to find out information critical and relevant to their success.

- Ad hoc teams receive enough resources to be successful.

- Training is provided for employees to build teamwork and collaboration skills (for example, running meetings, resolving conflicts).

- Recognition and promotion systems give significant weight to effectiveness in collaborating with others.

- Recognition and promotion decisions are based in part on a person's demonstrated initiative and results in pursuing new product or service opportunities.

- Key metrics on the organizational scorecard include leading indicators like the development of future capabilities.

- Reward systems take into account a unit's contribution to the broader enterprise as well as more specific measures of unit performance.

- Leadership development is systematically supported via multiple sorts of experiences including training, coaching, mentoring, action-learning projects, and developmental assignments.

- Talent management and succession-planning processes are integrated with leadership development experiences and tied to business strategy.

What Does This Mean for You?

You can apply these ideas about organizational culture, structure, and systems in two different ways. One has to do with understanding the conditions in your own organization and adapting your behavior to those conditions. The other deals with what you can do to help change the culture, structure, and systems in your organization to better support strategy as a learning process.

What Can I Do Now?

Your first challenge will be to assess your familiarity and confidence level with your current organizational environment. As you practice strategic thinking, acting, and influencing skills, keep that in mind and acknowledge when circumstances in your organization create obstacles to exercising strategic leadership the way you'd like. For example, your own boss and the broader organization may constrain your ability to act decisively in the face of uncertainty. In a similar vein, there may be limits to your opportunity to experiment. In general, the more similar your organization's culture, structure, and systems are to those optimal for making strategy a learning process, the better you'll be able to practice and develop strategic leadership on the job.

But even if your organization presents an optimal situation for practicing and developing strategic leadership skills, select just a few behaviors or skills to work on first. Don't overextend yourself by attempting too much change with too many goals.

How Can I Help Change My Organization?

Many managers become discouraged at times about how much impact they seem to have on their organizations. Even senior executives recognize the limited scope of their responsibilities and potential impact relative, for example, to the CEO's. On the other hand, all the leaders in an organization have the potential for having impact with intentional, specific initiatives in their own spheres of influence. In doing this they can model steps of making strategy a learning process.

You can also foster change by asking probing questions of other leaders in your organization: Have you considered this? Could you help me understand our strategy better? What are our two or three most important drivers of strategic success?

Following are some questions you can ask to assess your organization's current effectiveness and opportunities for making strategy a learning process:

- *Assessing where we are*. How timely and insightful is your assessment of your competitive environment? Do you and others know what your major competitors are doing? What new competition might be on the horizon? How effective are your processes for scanning the environment, and is information about your strategic situation collected and disseminated effectively to all who need to know? Is your assessment of your competitive environment based on making common sense with others?

- *Understanding who we are and where we want to go.* Are your organizational aspirations clear to you and others? Are you and others clear about your own aspirations for your part of the organization? What do you stand for—and what won't you stand for? What big goal are you collectively striving toward? Is it one that others embrace, that touches their hearts as well as their heads? What is your vision? Can you paint a compelling picture for others of your ideal future?

- *Learning how to get there.* What are your organizational processes for making strategy? Who is involved? Does it only flow down from the top, or does it also rise from the bottom? Does your process of strategy formulation reflect a process of progressive discovery, of ever-deeper insights and refinements? Are you clear about what the key strategic drivers are for your organization—those few factors that will exert the greatest leverage on your long-term success?

- *Making the journey.* How well are your tactics integrated with your strategy? Is there a clear link? What are your processes for making strategic decisions and executing the strategy? Is there appropriate emphasis on long-term as well as short-term outcomes?

- *Checking our progress.* Does your organization use some kind of balanced scorecard to assess organizational performance? What are your metrics for current performance? How do you assess your progress in developing future capability? What does success, or sustainable competitive advantage, look like? What form does it take? Is making and implementing strategy in your organization a continuing cycle? Does it deepen strategic insight and fine-tune execution? When you reassess where you are, do you look at your organization in the context of your broader competitive environment and whether it has changed? Have you changed?

The Role of Leadership Strategy in Making Strategy a Learning Process

When people talk about their organization's strategy, they usually refer to their company's pattern of business choices intended to enhance its sustainable competitive advantage. Oftentimes, however, organizations fail to give sufficient attention to their leadership strategy—the organizational and human capabilities needed to enact the business strategy effectively.

Leadership strategy represents an organization's strategic intent about leadership, including its philosophy, values, and general approach to leadership and leadership development. Leadership strategy encompasses matters of organizational values and culture as well as the role of systems in facilitating leadership and leadership development throughout the organization. It also includes the organization's strategy for developing the effectiveness of individual leaders and strategic leadership teams, which could include such components as training, coaching, mentoring, action learning, developmental assignments, multirater feedback, and team building.

Ironically, relatively few organizations have mastered how to develop and encourage the behavior of individuals and teams that are most likely to drive the organization toward enduring success. But individual managers can identify and encourage those behaviors themselves.

Improving Your Organization's Leadership Strategy

Following are several high-level ideas for improving your organization's leadership strategy. They represent general activities rather than specific exercises; you can adapt them to suit your needs in your own particular organizational environment.

These ideas are high-level in another sense as well. Their effectiveness depends on the active support of your senior team. Whether you are or are not part of your organization's top strategic leadership team, helping the organization move in this direction will be an opportunity for you to practice the role of champion for strategic change. At a minimum, you can use these guidelines as the framework for a conversation that you can initiate with others in the organization—perhaps your boss or someone in a human resources position. Such conversations can contribute significantly to the development of your own strategic leadership, and perhaps to theirs as well.

Clarify your organizational aspirations and current business strategy:

- Does your organization have a compelling vision? Does it have a clear mission? Does it espouse values that people accept and embrace?
- Are your senior team and other leaders in your organization clear about your organization's key strategic drivers?
- Assess the current understanding of your organization's business strategy throughout the workforce.
- Identify improvements to the process of strategy development, dissemination, and ongoing refinement that will best promote widespread understanding and commitment.

Identify the organizational and human capabilities needed to implement the business strategy effectively:

- Your organization is unlikely to have something actually called a leadership strategy. But most organizations have an implicit one even if there's no explicit version. You may need to do some research and investigation to discover its various elements.
- Clarify how changes in your competitive environment are calling for new kinds of organizational capabilities and what they are.

- Identify the implications for how leadership may need to be practiced differently in the organization as a result of these new competitive challenges and new capabilities.
- What capabilities, in particular, will be needed to support the prospect of continuing organizational change and the ongoing individual, team, and organizational learning it requires?

Assess the current state of capabilities needed
to implement the strategy effectively:

- Assess your organizational culture and identify any changes that may be needed in the light of new competitive challenges.
- Identify aspects of structure and systems that undercut the willingness or ability of individuals and teams to implement the strategy effectively. Minimize or eliminate such barriers, and implement other changes to encourage and reinforce strategic behavior by individuals and teams.
- Review mechanisms by which individuals and teams maintain a strategic perspective amid tactical, day-to-day demands.
- Do systems exist for adequately attracting, developing, and retaining the talent needed for success?

Make leadership development a key component
of your organization's leadership strategy:

- Identify the leadership competencies that are most critical to the success of your organization and its business strategy.
- Create a leadership development strategy incorporating multiple types of experiences: training, coaching, mentoring, action learning, and job assignments made intentionally for their developmental value. As much as possible, tailor specific leadership development experiences to individual needs and goals. Developmental experiences have the greatest impact when they are connected directly and continually with actual

work and when regular feedback about progress toward developmental goals is part of the experience.

- Create a feedback-rich environment for development, including regular opportunities for 360-degree feedback (feedback about one's leadership effectiveness from bosses, peers, direct reports, oneself, and in some cases other key stakeholders).

- Provide opportunities for developing the effectiveness of strategic leadership teams as well as for individual leader development.

Get top leadership support:

- Clarify the extent to which your top team sees leadership as a strategic competitive advantage for the organization.

- Enlist members of the senior team as public champions of leadership and leadership development.

- Create and execute a communication plan for making the linkage between your leadership strategy and business strategy better understood throughout the organization.

A Final Thought

This chapter focuses on what you can do to help make strategy a learning process throughout your organization. It discusses your part in fostering conditions in your organization in which individuals and teams can most effectively enact strategic thinking, acting, and influencing.

But perhaps that seems like too tall an order. Maybe you're thinking, "All that sounds fine, but you've got me confused with someone with real authority here, someone with the power to make things happen. I'm just one manager in a very large organization, and I have no control whatsoever over our culture or structure or systems."

Reactions like this are natural and sensible. Decisions about initiating major organizational changes typically rest with the top team, if not exclusively with the CEO. But that doesn't mean others throughout the organization have no opportunity at all to promote such change or influence more senior leaders.

You can do so in a number of ways. One is by simply raising issues with your own boss. You can ask questions about potentially counterproductive aspects of current dimensions of culture and systems (while also being savvy enough to acknowledge the positive reasons they may have evolved as well). Many senior executives have not thought systematically about the relationship between business strategy and leadership strategy, and you can play a helpful role in raising their awareness about the importance of having the supportive culture and systems that produce the desired results over the long term. The spirit of this conversation should not be that there is something wrong with the current situation. Rather, it should be in the spirit of exploring whether any different organizational conditions could be the foundation for attaining higher levels of sustainable competitive advantage.

Another thing you can do is intentionally create new behavioral practices or processes within your area of responsibility, and then share the results and practices that work best more broadly throughout your organization.

Although impact on the broader organization may seem "above your pay grade," such outcomes could well be some of your greatest contributions as a strategic leader. This chapter primarily addresses organization-level variables, but responsibility for change inevitably falls to the individual leader and to members of strategic leadership teams. In Chapter Seven we outline specific steps for becoming that more effective strategic leader.

Chapter Seven

Becoming a Strategic Leader

The preceding chapter focuses on conditions that help make strategy a learning process in your organization. The more such conditions exist, the more resources you will have to support your own development as a strategic leader. But since this book's primary purpose is to help you, we conclude by returning to a more personal focus. This chapter offers a few final suggestions about how to best ride the wave of leadership development. Our surfing metaphor suits us well here because the most powerful forms of strategic leadership development involve choosing experiences rich in opportunities for learning (picking the right wave) and learning all you can from them (riding it as far as you can).

Developing Your Strategic Leadership Is a Learning Process

As a framework for this discussion we return to the simplified version of the familiar model for strategy as a learning process (Figure 7.1). Its elements are also applicable to individual development and can be applied to the process of becoming a strategic leader.

Assessing Where You Are

In Chapter Two we discuss SWOT analysis, a common way of assessing an organization's strategic situation. You can apply a similar idea to assessing your own leadership development needs. You've probably done something like this before, without thinking

Figure 7.1. Developing Strategic Leadership.

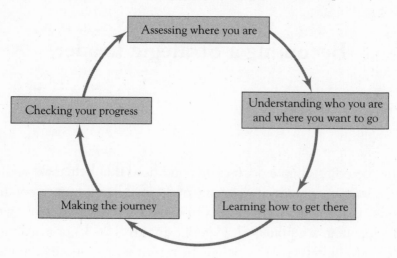

of it in these terms. A "personal SWOT" involves taking stock of your strengths and weaknesses as a leader and the opportunities and threats facing your future effectiveness. (Think of your future effectiveness in your present role as well as roles in different contexts that involve new challenges.)

Identify and Collect Relevant Data. To do a personal SWOT analysis, begin by identifying all the sources of data you have available concerning your present and future effectiveness as a strategic leader. Data you might collect include performance appraisals, developmental feedback at work, instrument-based assessments of leadership styles and preferences, current leadership challenges and opportunities in your work environment and how they might change over time (thus changing the relative importance of different competencies to your future effectiveness as a strategic leader), and the self-assessments in this book.

Exhibit 7.1 lists the items in the self-assessments for strategic thinking, acting, and influencing previously presented in Exhibits

2.3, 3.1, and 4.1. This will let you overview all the competencies you rated higher and lower within the respective thinking, acting, and influencing domains (or those needing relatively more or less improvement). It also will make it easier for you to look across those domains to explore more subtle interrelationships among them. For example, we've noted that it's important to be decisive in the face of uncertainty. Many times, however, it's important to make common sense before acting—especially when the situation is ambiguous. It would clearly be unhelpful if the impact of decisive action were to decrease the very sort of input needed from others for effective strategic thinking. Therefore, complete the self-assessment items in Exhibit 7.1 mindful of the real-world complexity in which they're enacted.

Sort the Data into SWOT Categories. After collecting this data, sort it into the various SWOT categories:

- *Strengths*. In what aspects of strategic leadership do you do well? For example, are you relatively strongest in strategic thinking? Strategic acting? Strategic influencing? Which specific skills in each are your greatest strengths?
- *Weaknesses*. In what aspects of strategic leadership are you less effective?
- *Opportunities*. What present or potential situations at work— if you took advantage of them—could help you improve your effectiveness as a strategic leader? For example, are there committee assignments dealing with strategic issues, educational opportunities, developmental job assignments, or mentors available to you?
- *Threats*. What present or potential situations at work—if you failed to address them—pose a danger to your long-term success as a strategic leader in this organization? For example, might new organizational requirements to work more cross-functionally pose a personal challenge? Would a requirement

Exhibit 7.1. Comprehensive Assessment of Your Strategic Thinking, Acting, and Influencing Skills.

For each of these behaviors, use the following scale to assess your need to improve in that area. "Need to improve" represents the relative gap between your current competency and how good you *should* be.

1	2	3	4	5
Considerable Improvement Needed		Moderate Improvement Needed		No Improvement Needed

Strategic Thinking

Scan the environment for forces and trends that could impact the organization's competitiveness.

1   2   3   4   5

Ensure that all necessary information is considered.

1   2   3   4   5

See things in new and different ways.

1   2   3   4   5

Identify the truly key facts or trends amid the large amount of data available to be considered.

1   2   3   4   5

Understand your own biases and do not let them play too strong of a role in your thinking.

1   2   3   4   5

Identify key points or issues and discern the truly significant information among the explosion of data confronting you.

1   2   3   4   5

See patterns and relationships between seemingly disparate data, and ask probing questions about the interactive effects among various parts of the business.

1   2   3   4   5

Offer original, creative ideas.

1   2   3   4   5

Strategic Acting

Be decisive in the face of uncertainty.

       1   2   3   4   5

Manage the tension between success in daily tasks and success in the long term.

       1   2   3   4   5

Implement tactics consistent with strategy.

       1   2   3   4   5

Make decisions that are strategically consistent with each other.

       1   2   3   4   5

Facilitate others' actions by providing them a helpful balance of direction and autonomy.

       1   2   3   4   5

Find ways to reward appropriate risk-taking.

       1   2   3   4   5

Recognize the need to adapt existing plans to changing conditions.

       1   2   3   4   5

Learn from actions by deliberately reflecting on their consequences, and use such learning to inform future decisions and actions.

       1   2   3   4   5

Examine mistakes for their learning value (as opposed to apportioning blame).

       1   2   3   4   5

Strategic Influencing

Understand your impact on others and how that affects the quality of collective work.

       1   2   3   4   5

Build a network of relationships with people who are not part of the routine structure of your work.

       1   2   3   4   5

Exhibit 7.1. Comprehensive Assessment of Your Strategic Thinking, Acting, and Influencing Skills (*continued*).

Accurately assess the political landscape.

      1   2   3   4   5

Navigate the political landscape without limiting your credibility.

      1   2   3   4   5

Develop a compelling vision.

      1   2   3   4   5

Create enthusiasm and understanding about a vision of the future in the hearts and minds of others.

      1   2   3   4   5

Create ways to discuss the undiscussable.

      1   2   3   4   5

Ask questions of others' perspectives to deepen your own understanding of their view.

      1   2   3   4   5

Understand the needs, styles, and motivations of others, and use that information to communicate with them and influence them.

      1   2   3   4   5

Create champions throughout the organization to further your project or cause.

      1   2   3   4   5

Use aspirational language and stories to draw people to your concepts.

      1   2   3   4   5

Celebrate and advertise successes to build and sustain momentum.

      1   2   3   4   5

Be open to influence from others.

      1   2   3   4   5

for using feedback from peers or direct reports in the performance appraisal process be an obstacle?

Finally, don't forget to assess the strengths, weaknesses, opportunities, and threats facing your strategic leadership team too. Use the SWOT format outlined above to help you do that.

Understanding Who You Are and Where You Want to Go

What are your personal aspirations as a leader? What kind of leader do you want to be? It may be useful to translate these broad questions into four related areas:

- *Values*. What values are most central and critical to how you approach work? What values do you want to be known for *practicing* (not just preaching)?
- *Leadership legacy*. What do you want to be your leadership legacy to others? What do you want others to say about your leadership after you've left your current position or the organization? What lasting impact do you want to have—not just on the organization but also on the people around you?
- *Career aspirations*. What kind of role would you like to have five or ten years from now? Describe the critical elements of what for you would be an ideal opportunity for strategic leadership.
- *Aspirations for your SLT*. What are your aspirations for your strategic leadership team? How would you like others to describe the way your team provides strategic leadership to the organization? What is your vision for the kind of strategic impact you'd like your team to have?

Learning How to Get There

Leadership development is a process, one that depends on your ability and willingness to learn from your experience. Although that seems obvious, CCL's long-term research project into the lessons of experience indicates that not all executives learn equally well from their experiences, even if they have quite similar ones (for example, Leslie & Van Velsor, 1996; McCall, Lombardo, & Morrison, 1988).

What Kinds of Experiences and Attitudes Best Develop Leadership Skills? It's clear from research that some experiences are developmentally richer and more powerful than others. That's probably consistent with your own experience. When managers and executives are asked what two or three events throughout their careers contributed the most to making them the kind of leaders they are today, their responses tend to fall into a very few categories such as challenging assignments and learning from others. What's also required is a willingness to go against the grain of one's habitual behavior when confronted with a new challenge.

Figure 7.2 depicts what we call the "going against the grain" response. It helps to explain why people often avoid acting in ways most likely to enhance their learning. Learning by definition involves doing something differently than you have before. Ironically, it's precisely when new challenges call for new behaviors that many managers and executives are least willing to experiment with new behaviors. That's because going against the grain almost always involves a short-term decrement in effectiveness, even though it offers the chance of long-term improvement.

Getting out of your rut requires a willingness to make mistakes and demonstrate less competence in a new behavior than you might have in a much more practiced behavior. But keep in mind that the more practiced behavior—one of your strengths—precludes learning and improved effectiveness in the long term. The risk of going against the grain pays off in its potential, as described in this summary of CCL's lessons of experience research:

> What did seem to characterize the successful executives we studied was not their genetic endowment nor even their impressive array of life experience. Rather, as a group, they seemed ready to grab or create opportunities for growth, wise enough not to believe that there's

Figure 7.2. The "GAG" Response: Going against the Grain.

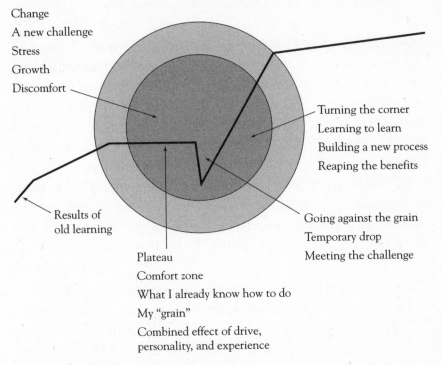

Change
A new challenge
Stress
Growth
Discomfort

Turning the corner
Learning to learn
Building a new process
Reaping the benefits

Results of
old learning

Going against the grain
Temporary drop
Meeting the challenge

Plateau
Comfort zone
What I already know how to do
My "grain"
Combined effect of drive,
personality, and experience

nothing more to learn, and courageous enough to look inside themselves and grapple with their frailties. Not only could they do these things, they also seemed able to do them under the worst possible conditions: handling a crisis when just getting the job done demanded their full attention and all of their energy; when other people, bosses and subordinates alike, were waiting for them to prove themselves; when personal catastrophe struck; when major forces over which they had no control were dictating events; when no one knew what was happening, much less what to do about it; when they were disappointed or frustrated or victimized.

So if there is indeed a right stuff for executives it may be this extraordinary tenacity in extracting something worthwhile from their experience and in seeking experiences rich in opportunities for growth (McCall, Lombardo, & Morrison, 1988, p. 122).

Identify Your Own Developmental Strategic Drivers. Throughout this book we emphasize the importance of understanding the key strategic drivers of your organization's success. In an analogous way it is helpful to understand the key drivers of your own strategic leadership effectiveness. Using information from your personal SWOT analysis and aspirations, try to identify the three or four things most critical to your success as a strategic leader.

Developmental drivers are closely related to individual or team development objectives, but there are usually more objectives than drivers since multiple objectives can be derived from one driver. Here are a few examples of each, with the drivers in italic:

- *Engage others in strategic discussions in ways that leverage their perspectives and insights and create shared meaning and ownership of the outcomes.* One objective based on this driver could be to develop skill in facilitating meetings dealing with ambiguous and ill-defined problems. Another could be to develop and reinforce team norms that emphasize building upon others' ideas rather than trying to come up with the "best" idea yourself.

- *Develop agility to respond in a more timely and strategic way to rapidly changing situations.* One objective based on this driver could be to develop competence in creating alternate possible future scenarios. Another could be to delegate aspects of strategic leadership to groups situated closer to the changing situations (for example, in field offices).

- *Develop a team climate, commitment, and set of norms that facilitate progressive strategic learning, both collectively and individually.* One objective based on this driver could be for your strategic leadership team to conduct a process debriefing after major phases of its work (for example, What can we learn from this experience that will help us be more effective next time?). Another could be to share and support individual leadership development goals among members of the team.

Making the Journey

Making the journey is about the tactics needed to implement a strategy effectively. In this case it's about the specific actions needed to achieve your aspirations.

Create a Development Plan. It's now time to create your development plan. Most organizations have their own specific formats for these, so we will just highlight some of the key elements here. Development plans should include your long-term aspirations; your immediate developmental objectives; the specific actions you'll take to achieve your objectives, particularly in your choice of developmental experiences; the resources and support you'll need on that developmental journey; a timeline for achieving your objectives; and appropriate metrics or success measures by which you'll know that you have accomplished what you intended.

Select Experiences to Leverage Your Developmental Drivers. In many ways the most critical elements of your development plan are the experiences from which you intend to learn. These experiences are the cauldron of learning, and they vary in many ways: in terms of how much challenge they pose, given your present levels of skill and experience, in the domain of learning engaged (cognitive or interpersonal, for example), and in the consequences associated with succeeding or failing in the activity. Here are just a few of the kinds of experiences you might consider as part of your own plan to develop your strategic leadership:

- Opportunities to better understand the competitive environment—following market trends, market research, and so forth

- Projects to review aspects of corporate aspirations (values, culture, climate)
- Development, implementation, and interpretation of your company's strategic metrics (for example, developing a new balanced scorecard)
- Strategic planning—translating strategy and goals into operational plans and tactics, scenario planning
- Work assignments that span accustomed corporate boundaries (cross-functional, cross-regional, and so on)
- Observing and assisting key strategic leadership teams
- Enterprise-wide communication initiatives to promote shared understanding and alignment around the strategy
- Working on an action-learning team tasked to come up with a new solution to a vexing problem
- Writing an article for a corporate publication on some aspect of corporate strategy, direction, or other attribute
- Serving on a task force to identify critical organizational capabilities for success in the next decade
- Opportunities to assist or observe very senior strategic leadership teams

Create Support for Yourself.   We've noted how risky it can feel to go against the grain, especially when the stakes of success and failure are high. Asking successful people to tackle new behaviors and risk failing is asking a lot. That's precisely why some of the most important resources to include in your development plan are ways to support yourself during your learning. Such support can include technical resources (written materials on leading virtual teams, for example) as well as socioemotional support (perhaps a coach or confidant with whom you can seek guidance, vent, or engage in developmental conversations).

Be Vigilant for Emergent Development Opportunities.   Creating a development plan is a good idea, but don't let the existence of the plan distract your attention from ways that unforeseen opportunities might represent even better ways to leverage your own developmental drivers.

Checking Your Progress

Your development plan will identify critical milestones of your progress. As was the case with strategic business drivers, however, these might change over time. Don't let your development plan or objectives become ends in themselves. Regularly reassess whether the drivers you've identified continue to be the most critical ones for your own long-term development.

Your development cycle continues in an iterative fashion as your progressive development creates opportunities for leadership requiring different skills and further development. This idea may be made clearest to you by looking back over the years at your own career and development. What, for example, were the greatest lessons about leadership you learned on your very first job? Did you learn different lessons in subsequent positions, facing different situations and maybe working with different people? Looking back, you can see your ongoing development in terms of repeated loops of strategic leadership as a learning process. Each loop represents a successive cycle of learning occurring across different jobs you've held or across different stages of your career.

Closing Words

Our primary reason for writing this book was to give managers and executives a more personal perspective about what it means to be strategic as a leader, as well as suggestions about how to become one. But this book does not make becoming a strategic leader easy. You cannot develop by reading a book, pushing a button, or filling a square.

Strategic leadership is a bit like surfing. Both involve keeping your balance while learning the best path to follow amid constantly changing conditions. Your challenge now is to start moving on the path to more effective strategic leadership by developing your own and your team's thinking, acting, and influencing skills. This also happens to be your primary role in ensuring your organization's enduring success.

Appendix A

Strategic Driver Paired-Voting Form

In the paired voting for each cell, record the number of votes for the driver listed in the far left-hand column.

Strategic Driver	A	B	C	D	E	F	G	H	I	J
A										
B										
C										
D										
E										
F										
G										
H										
I										
J										

Appendix B

STRAT: Strategic Team Review and Action Tool

You have been chosen to survey a strategic leadership team of which you are a member. The phrase *strategic leadership team* (SLT) refers to those individuals who collectively exert significant influence on the strategic direction of a particular business unit, product line, function (product development, engineering, marketing, and so on), division, or company. SLTs need not be explicitly designated or chartered, can include individuals with varying authority relationships, and can range from four to more than twenty members. The SLT you are to survey may comprise a combination of direct reports, peers you work with often, and people you rarely work with directly.

The Strategic Team Review and Action Tool (STRAT) consists of questions designed to survey a strategic leadership team within an organization. Your task, as a recipient of this survey, is to complete it by answering the questions as they relate to the SLT defined for you. The results of this survey will help you and the members of the SLT analyze strategic leadership in that team and the overall company. A list of the members and observer groups of this SLT has been included with the cover letter for your reference.

The name of the SLT you are to survey is printed in the space indicated on the next page. Complete the STRAT survey questions responding to the items as they apply to that strategic leadership team. Please be open and candid in your responses. The report will show a summary of the group's responses. Your individual responses will not be identifiable to anyone else.

Print this survey and complete it using a blue or black pen. Return it on or before the due date.

Thank you.

STRAT—Strategic Team Review and Action Tool

YOUR NAME: _____

Due Date:

SLT NAME: [preprinted when survey is in use]

Please respond to the survey items as they apply to the strategic leadership team named above.
For each item, select one option by circling a number to show how much you agree or disagree that the statement describes this SLT, using the following scale:

5 = Strongly Agree	4 = Agree	3 = Neutral	2 = Disagree	1 = Strongly Disagree

5 4 3 2 1   1. This strategic leadership team regularly and realistically assesses its organizational strengths and weaknesses.

5 4 3 2 1   2. This strategic leadership team understands the threats and opportunities in the external environment.

5 4 3 2 1   3. This strategic leadership team has a shared vision of our future.

5 4 3 2 1   4. Individuals at all levels understand how their roles support the organizational mission.

5 4 3 2 1   5. This strategic leadership team keeps abreast of technological, cultural, and market trends.

5 4 3 2 1   6. This strategic leadership team is clear about our basic purpose and core values.

5 4 3 2 1   7. This strategic leadership team thinks globally.

5 4 3 2 1   8. This strategic leadership team encourages others to improve by experimenting with new or different ways of doing things.

5 4 3 2 1   9. There are few undiscussable subjects here.

#	Statement					
10.	Different opinions are welcome.	5	4	3	2	1
11.	Our strategy is discriminating: clear about what we *will* do and clear about what we *will not* do.	5	4	3	2	1
12.	This strategic leadership team works well together.	5	4	3	2	1
13.	This strategic leadership team is composed of diverse individuals with complementary talents.	5	4	3	2	1
14.	This strategic leadership team shares information well with each other.	5	4	3	2	1
15.	Members of this strategic leadership team have constructive interactions with others throughout the organization.	5	4	3	2	1
16.	This strategic leadership team actively supports executive growth and development.	5	4	3	2	1
17.	Getting ahead here depends upon performance, not politics.	5	4	3	2	1
18.	This strategic leadership team strikes an appropriate balance between dealing with short-term and long-term needs.	5	4	3	2	1
19.	This strategic leadership team encourages an appropriate level of risk-taking.	5	4	3	2	1
20.	This strategic leadership team does not waste its own or others' energy on unproductive activities.	5	4	3	2	1
21.	This strategic leadership team responds effectively to opportunities and threats in the environment.	5	4	3	2	1
22.	Members of this strategic leadership team trust and respect each other.	5	4	3	2	1
23.	This strategic leadership team fosters cooperation rather than competition across organizational units.	5	4	3	2	1
24.	We share best practices across individuals and departments.	5	4	3	2	1
25.	This strategic leadership team exhibits a high level of integrity.	5	4	3	2	1
26.	I am proud of the way this strategic leadership team handles issues of right or wrong.	5	4	3	2	1
27.	There is a positive sense of energy and excitement around here.	5	4	3	2	1

Appendix C

STRAT Items and
the Learning Process

Assessing where we are

1. This SLT regularly and realistically assesses its organizational strengths and weaknesses.
2. This SLT understands the threats and opportunities in the external environment.
5. This SLT keeps abreast of technological, cultural, and market trends.

General SLT Effectiveness

7. This SLT thinks globally.
9. There are few undiscussable subjects here.
10. Different opinions are welcome.
12. This SLT works well together.
13. This SLT is composed of diverse individuals with complementary talents.
14. This SLT shares information well with each other.
22. Members of this SLT trust and respect each other.
25. This SLT exhibits a high level of integrity.
26. I am proud of the way this SLT handles issues of right or wrong.

Understanding who we are and where we want to go

3. This SLT has a shared vision of our future.
6. This SLT is clear about our basic purpose and core values.

Learning how to get there

Business Strategy

11. Our strategy is discriminating: clear about what we will do and clear about what we will not do.

Leadership Strategy

8. This SLT encourages others to improve by experimenting with new or different ways of doing things.
15. Members of this SLT have constructive interactions with others throughout the organization.
16. This SLT actively supports executive growth and development.
17. Getting ahead here depends upon performance, not politics.
19. This SLT encourages an appropriate level of risk-taking.
23. This SLT fosters cooperation rather than competition across organizational units.
24. We share best practices across individuals and departments.
27. There is a positive sense of energy and excitement around here.

Making the journey

4. Individuals at all levels understand how their roles support the organizational mission.
18. This SLT strikes an appropriate balance between dealing with short-term and long-term needs.
20. This SLT does not waste its own or others' energy on unproductive activities.
21. This SLT responds effectively to opportunities and threats in the environment.

Appendix D

Using STRAT to Develop Your SLT

The purpose of STRAT is to generate conversation among SLT members regarding what they are doing well and what they could do better. It is not a validated instrument, which means it is not appropriate to say that teams that score higher on STRAT are necessarily better than teams that score lower. Rather than use it as a measurement, we suggest you use it as a springboard for conversations regarding team processes.

If you are not the leader of the team, you'll need to gain agreement ahead of time to use STRAT. Spend some time talking with the leader about STRAT and the role of teams in the strategic leadership of the organization. Perhaps you have already had conversations about this particular SLT and discussed what is working well and what is not. Be prepared to answer questions such as these:

- Why should this SLT go through a process like this?
- Why this tool versus another tool?
- Why now?
- What is the benefit of this process?

Typically, the process of using STRAT involves three steps. First, you'll need to prepare the team for the tool and distribute it for completion. Next, the results must be scored so that the team can make sense of them. Finally, the results will need to be reviewed with the team.

Step 1: Preparing the Team and Distributing STRAT

Spend some time before handing out the STRAT tool to prepare the team. A few steps such as the following will go a long way toward ensuring the successful use of STRAT.

- Determine exactly who will complete STRAT. If all team members can complete it, the data will have more meaning because people will not think, "I understand the results, but I wonder whether everyone feels this way." Similarly, all members can then feel that they have had input into the data and can participate fully in the conversations regarding the results and any actions taken as a result of those conversations. In terms of protecting the team members' confidentiality, more inputs are better. In fact, we recommend you require a minimum of three or four people complete STRAT so that no one can determine the others' responses with certainty.

- Make sure the team members know the team leader's reasons for using STRAT at this point in time. Encourage the team leader—if it is someone other than yourself—to communicate with team members regarding that rationale.

- Make sure that all members are rating the same SLT. If your team has a name, include that in the copies of STRAT that are distributed. It's very important that everyone thinks about the same team when they make their ratings.

- When you distribute STRAT, let members know that their individual ratings will be kept confidential and that no one on the team will see any other individual's ratings. Assign a trusted and objective person (who is not a member of the team) to collect the STRAT forms and produce the summary of the ratings.

- Ask members to be as honest as possible when making their ratings so that the team can benefit most fully from this experience.

- Suggest that the members keep a copy of their own individual ratings since you will not return that data to them. It can be very helpful in the discussion of the results if people remember their own individual ratings (even though they will not be asked to share those ratings).

- Finally, give a deadline for the return of STRAT. Typically, it takes fifteen to twenty minutes to complete the tool. Most people should be able to find time to complete it within a week. Ask that individuals return it to your assigned person by the deadline.

- Ask your assigned person to follow up with people to ensure that the forms are collected.

Step 2: Scoring STRAT

STRAT provides two general types of data that will be helpful in examining the team's results:

- Average ratings for each item. Ask your assigned person to average the ratings across all the members for each item and to provide that information in a report format. The report will be most helpful if it can list the item number, item text, and the average rating. Additionally, if the average ratings can be sorted from highest to lowest it will be easier to review the data.

- Frequency distribution for each item. While an average is helpful, it does not tell how dispersed the ratings are. For example, an average of 3 can be produced in different ways: everyone gives the item a 3, or half the respondents give it a 1 and half give it a 5 (among other possibilities). Those two scenarios are quite different; the second one suggests there is a fair amount of disagreement among members regarding that item. A frequency distribution shows how many people gave the item a 1, how many a 2, how many a 3, and so on. It is very helpful when assessing team agreement or disagreement on a particular item.

Reporting frequency distributions poses a slight risk, particularly if the team is small, because it may cause members to ask, "Who gave this a 2?" One way to minimize this risk and still provide the information about agreement or disagreement is simply to flag those items where there is a gap of three or more points between the highest and lowest ratings. (For example, the lowest rating is a 2 and the highest rating is a 5, or the lowest rating is a 1 and the highest rating is a 4.) You might want to use this method rather than the frequency distribution if your team has five or fewer members.

Step 3: Debriefing STRAT

Once everyone has completed the tool and your assigned person has produced a summary of the results, it is time to sit down with the team to review those results. The following two sections give some suggestions regarding that meeting.

General Tips for Debriefing STRAT with Your SLT

- Consider using an outside facilitator, particularly if you are the leader of the SLT. Facilitation requires a level of objectivity that is very difficult to maintain as a team member or team leader. Additionally, having another person present to focus on the facilitation allows you to participate more fully in the conversations about the team.
- Ensure that you have enough time to discuss the results and take some action based on that discussion. Allow three hours minimum for this conversation, more if this type of conversation is new for your team or if you have significant issues on the team.

- Consider holding the meeting off-site to minimize distractions and allow people more opportunity for reflection. Also, ask people to turn off cell phones, pagers, laptops, PDAs, and other distracting devices.

- Set norms at the outset of the meeting to encourage respect for confidentiality and exploration of multiple perspectives. Focus on the issues, not on who said what. Here are some helpful norms to include:

  Speak to your own data and do not ask others to share their scores on particular items. (Of course, people can share their scores, but that sharing should be initiated by them.)

  When there is a confusing data point, consider it a paradox to be understood and not an anomaly that must be incorrect just because it is different from the others. Do this by hypothesizing in the following way: "If I had answered this item in this way, I would have been thinking about the ways in which we . . ."

- Inevitably, the group will get into a discussion of what they have control over because several of the STRAT items have root causes that may exist outside the team. This is particularly true if the team is not the top management team in the organization. The danger in these discussions is that the team will feel helpless to do anything to improve the situation. However, encourage them to keep two things in mind:

  It is possible to separate out what the team does have control over from what it does not have control over. In fact, put the two sets of items on separate presentation charts to provide a visual cue as to the differences. Encourage team members to focus their action planning on those items over which they do have control.

  Items they don't have control over provide members with an opportunity to influence people outside the team. For example, if members feel that the organization's strategy is not discriminating enough and that this is leading to a situation where the team is not clear regarding what it should and should not be doing, they can generate a list of clarifying questions and take that list to the top management team.

Possible Flow of a STRAT Debriefing Meeting

If you are facilitating a meeting to debrief the STRAT results, this description of a meeting can help you set the pace. These activities are not inclusive of everything you might do, but they have worked well for us in our work with strategic leadership teams.

- If the team is unfamiliar with strategic leadership concepts and the implications those have for the team, consider assigning some advance reading, such as this book or selected chapters of this book. Even if members are familiar with strategic leadership in general, providing a framework gives everyone a common language to use when discussing their strengths and challenges.

- Begin the meeting with an icebreaker. For example, ask the team members to each share what they believe their own role on the team is. Examples include devil's advocate and integrator. Also ask team members to share their expectations for the meeting.

- Frame the purpose of the day. Your purpose might be to generate discussion about how team members are working together, to see whether the team wants to change anything about its interactions and its effectiveness as a strategic leadership team, and, if so, to set plans in place to make those changes.

- Set some norms for the meeting as discussed earlier.

- Have a discussion about what is important for the team to do effectively, given the nature of the challenges it faces. One possible way to do this is to provide a list of the STRAT items to members and ask each member to pick the three to five they feel are most critical to the success of the team. Summarize the items and record them on a presentation chart. The team members will be tempted to discuss all twenty-seven STRAT items, but this list will help them narrow their focus.

- Hand back the STRAT aggregate data and explain how to read it.

- It might also be helpful for members to have some comparison data. (The norm data that CCL has collected for STRAT appears in Appendix E.)

- Allow time for members to study the data and to reflect on what they see.

- Ask each person to complete the following sentences. They might have more than one way to complete each one. Each version should be placed on a separate note.

  I am pleased that the data shows our strengths are . . .

  When I look at the data, I am confused by . . .

  Given what is important to this team, I think we need to focus on improving . . .

- Put up a piece of presentation chart paper for each sentence starter. Ask members to place their notes on the appropriate chart paper.

- Divide the group into three smaller groups and ask each group to take one sentence. Their task is to summarize the responses to it by generating the common themes they see in the notes.

- Have the group that summarizes the strengths report first.

- Next, have the group that summarizes the confusing points share its report. Leave some time for discussion.

- Finally, have the group that summarizes the areas for improvement share its report. As part of the discussion, consider the overlap between the sentences. For example:

> Are the areas where we have confusion contributing to our challenges as a team?
>
> Are there ways we could build upon our strengths to help with the challenges we have?
>
> Is there any way we are overusing a strength, so that it might be working against us?

- Once there is agreement about the categories under areas for improvement, have a discussion about the root causes of the issues. One simple way to do this is to use the "five why's" technique. That is, ask yourselves, "Why is this happening?" five times, each time building on the preceding answer.

- Generate as many as three goals you would like to set for yourselves.

- Assign a champion to each goal, a person who will take the lead to ensure that the group addresses the goal. The champion may need to convene a smaller group to do some work off-line.

- Discuss the next steps for the team.

Appendix E

STRAT Norm Data

Rank	Average	Std. Dev.	STRAT Question Ranked by Average (Highest to Lowest)
1	4.20	0.74	25. This strategic leadership team exhibits a high level of integrity.
2	4.15	0.70	13. This strategic leadership team is composed of diverse individuals with complementary talents.
3	4.07	0.81	6. This strategic leadership team is clear about our basic purpose and core values.
4	4.00	0.83	26. I am proud of the way this strategic leadership team handles issues of right or wrong.
5	3.94	0.79	2. This strategic leadership team understands the threats and opportunities in the external environment.
6	3.93	0.86	10. Different opinions are welcome.
7	3.89	0.83	12. This strategic leadership team works well together.
8	3.89	0.75	15. Members of this strategic leadership team have constructive interactions with others throughout the organization.
9	3.82	0.91	22. Members of this strategic leadership team trust and respect each other.
10	3.81	0.87	23. This strategic leadership team fosters cooperation rather than competition across organizational units.
11	3.77	0.81	5. This strategic leadership team keeps abreast of technological, cultural, and market trends.
12	3.75	0.92	3. This strategic leadership team has a shared vision of our future.
13	3.72	0.94	27. There is a positive sense of energy and excitement around here.
14	3.72	1.04	9. There are few undiscussable subjects here.
15	3.69	0.88	16. This strategic leadership team actively supports executive growth and development.
16	3.67	0.81	19. This strategic leadership team encourages an appropriate level of risk-taking.

		Mean	SD
17	21. This strategic leadership team responds effectively to opportunities and threats in the environment.	3.64	0.80
18	17. Getting ahead here depends upon performance, not politics.	3.61	0.98
19	1. This strategic leadership team regularly and realistically assesses its organizational strengths and weaknesses.	3.60	0.97
20	14. This strategic leadership team shares information well with each other.	3.59	0.92
21	8. This strategic leadership team encourages others to improve by experimenting with new or different ways of doing things.	3.59	0.92
22	24. We share best practices across individuals and departments.	3.57	0.92
23	4. Individuals at all levels understand how their roles support the organizational mission.	3.57	0.94
24	18. This strategic leadership team strikes an appropriate balance between dealing with short-term and long-term needs.	3.50	0.90
25	7. This strategic leadership team thinks globally.	3.42	1.02
26	11. Our strategy is discriminating: clear about what we *will* do and clear about what we *will not* do.	3.31	0.95
27	20. This strategic leadership team does not waste its own or others' energy on unproductive activities.	3.28	0.97

Frequency of Ratings Across All Items by This Group (Percentage)

5	4	3	2	1
18	50	21	10	1

References

Advice on strategy: Quotes quotations. (n.d.). Available online: http://www. adviceonmanagement.com/advice_strategy.html. Access date: June 30, 2004.

Ambrose, S. E. (1983). *Eisenhower: 1890–1952*. New York: Simon & Schuster.

Associated Press. (2004, May 16). Three die near Denver in I-70 girder collapse. *The Gazette* (Metro), p. 27.

Baird, L., Holland, P., & Deacon, S. (1999, Spring). Learning from action: Imbedding more learning into the performance process fast enough to make a difference. *Organizational Dynamics*, pp. 19–31.

Banham, R. (1999, August). The revolution in planning. CFO, pp. 46–56.

Beatty, K. (2003, January). Strategic leadership poll results. *CCL e-Newsletter*. Available online (with registration): https://www.ccl.org/CCLCommerce/ news/newsletters/enewsletter/2003/JANdecpollresults.aspx?CatalogID= News&CategoryID=Enewsletter(Newsletters). Access date: July 28, 2004.

Beer, M., & Eisenstat, R. (2000). The silent killers of strategy implementation and learning. *Sloan Management Review, 41*(4), 29–40.

Bossidy, L., & Charan, R. (2002). *Execution: The discipline of getting things done*. New York: Crown Business.

Bunker, K. A., & Webb, A. D. (1992). *Learning how to learn from experience: Impact of trust and coping*. Greensboro, NC: Center for Creative Leadership.

Campbell, A., & Alexander, M. (1997). What's wrong with strategy? *Harvard Business Review, 75*(6), 42–51.

Collins, J. (2001). *Good to great*. New York: Harper Business.

Courtney, H., Kirkland, J., & Viguerie, P. (1997). Strategy under uncertainty. *Harvard Business Review, 75*(6), 66–79.

Digital Equipment Corporation. (2004, July 25). *Wikipedia*. Available online: http://en.wikipedia.org/wiki/Digital_Equipment_Corporation. Access date: July 28, 2004.

Fiorina, C. (2000, June 2). *Whole person leadership*. Commencement address at Massachusetts Institute of Technology, Cambridge Massachusetts. Available online: http://www.hp.com/hpinfo/execteam/speeches/fiorina/ceo_ mit_commence.html. Access date: August 25, 2004.

Floyd, S. W., & Wooldridge, B. (1996). *The strategic middle manager: How to create and sustain competitive advantage*. San Francisco: Jossey-Bass.

Galpin, T., & Herndon, M. (1999). *The complete guide to mergers and acquisitions: Process tools to support M&A integration at every level*. San Francisco: Jossey-Bass.

Gerstner, L. (2002). *Who says elephants can't dance?* New York: HarperCollins.

Hammond, J. S., Keeney, R. L., & Raiffa, H. (1998). The hidden traps in decision making. *Harvard Business Review, 76*(5), 47–58.

Hendricks, K. B., & Singhal, V. R. (1997). Does implementing an effective TQM program actually improve operating performance? Empirical evidence from firms that have won quality awards. *Management Science, 43*(9), 1258–1274.

Iacocca, L., with Novak, W. (1984). *Iacocca: An autobiography*. New York: Bantam.

Item 182: The president's news conference of August 4, 1954. (1960). *Public papers of the presidents of the United States, Dwight D. Eisenhower, 1954: Containing the public messages, speeches, and statements of the presidents, January 1 to December 31, 1954* (p. 684). Washington, DC: GPO.

Kaplan, R. S., & Norton, D. P. (1996). *The balanced scorecard*. Boston: Harvard Business School Press.

Katzenbach, J. R. (1997). The myth of the top management team. *Harvard Business Review, 75*(6), 82–91.

Katzenbach, J. R. (1998). *Teams at the top: Unleashing the potential of both teams and individual leaders*. Boston: Harvard Business School Press.

Lazere, C. (1998, February). All together now: Why you must link budgeting and forecasting to planning and performance. *CFO*, pp. 28–36.

Leslie, J. B., & Van Velsor, E. (1996). *A look at derailment today: North America and Europe*. Greensboro, NC: Center for Creative Leadership.

Linkow, P. (1999). What gifted strategic leaders do. *Training and Development, 53*(7), 34–41.

Lynn, G. S., Morone, J. G., & Paulson, A. S. (1996). Marketing and discontinuous innovation: The probe and learn process. *California Management Review, 38*(3), 353–375.

McCall, M. W., Jr., Lombardo, M. M., & Morrison, A. M. (1988). *The lessons of experience: How successful executives develop on the job*. Lexington, MA: Lexington Books.

McCann, J. (2004). Organizational effectiveness: Changing concepts for changing environments. *Human Resource Planning, 27*(1), 42–50.

Mintzberg, H. (1987). Crafting strategy. *Harvard Business Review, 65*(4), 66–75.

Mintzberg, H. (1998). *Strategy safari*. New York: Free Press.

Mintzberg, H., & Waters, J. A. (1985). Of strategies, deliberate and emergent. *Strategic Management Journal, 6*, 257–272.

Montgomery, B. L. (1958). *Memoirs*. Cleveland: World.

Nadler, D. A. (1996). Managing the team at the top. *Strategy and Business, 2,* 42–51.

Nadler, D. A. (1998). Leading executive teams. In D. A. Nadler, J. L. Spencer, & Associates (Eds.), *Executive teams.* San Francisco: Jossey-Bass.

Palus, C. J., & Horth, D. M. (2002). *The leader's edge: Six creative competencies for navigating complex challenges.* San Francisco: Jossey-Bass.

Pfeffer, J. (1981). *Power in organizations.* Marshfield, MA: Pitman.

Porter, M. (1996). What is strategy? *Harvard Business Review, 74*(6), 61–78.

Powell, C., with Pirsico, J. (1995). *My American journey.* New York: Random House.

Richmond, B. (2000). *The "thinking" in systems thinking: Seven essential skills.* Waltham, MA: Pegasus Communications.

Salter, C. (2002, January). Fresh start 2002: On the road again. *Fast Company,* p. 50.

Sanders, T. I. (2002, May 5). To fight terror, we can't think straight. *Washington Post,* p. B12.

Senge, P. (1990). *The fifth discipline: The art and practice of the learning organization.* New York: Doubleday.

Stewart, T. (1999, February/March). The status of communication today: Organizational change dominates internal communication activity. *Strategic Communication Management,* pp. 22–25.

Storytelling that moves people: A conversation with screenwriting coach Robert McKee. (2003). *Harvard Business Review, 81*(6), 51–55.

Treacy, T., & Wiersema, F. (1995). *The discipline of market leaders.* Reading, MA: Addison-Wesley.

Wason, P. C. (1960). On the failure to eliminate hypotheses in a conceptual task. *Quarterly Journal of Experimental Psychology, 12,* 129–140.

Watson, T. J., Sr. (n.d.). *Quintessential quotes.* Available online: http://www-1.ibm.com/ibm/history/documents/pdf/quotes.pdf. Access date: June 28, 2004.

Welch, J. (2003). *Jack: Straight from the gut.* New York: Warner Business Books.

Zauderer, D. G. (1992, Fall). Integrity: An essential executive quality. *Business Forum,* pp. 12–16.

Index

A

Abeles, J., 76–77, 197–198
Action: learning from, 101–107; translating strategy into, 30. *See also* Strategic acting; Tactics
After-action review (AAR), 104–107
Agility: balancing direction and autonomy for, 96, 97–98; development of, 224; need for, 2, 96
Alexander, M., 102
Alignment. *See* Strategic alignment
Alternate futures, 112
Ambiguity: making common sense in, 67–68; of strategic change, 161–162; trend of, 2, 18; uncertainty and, 112
Ambrose, S. E., 110
American Power Conversion (APC), 147–149, 165–166
Analog Devices, 105–107
Analytic thinking: nonlinear thinking and, 46–47; *versus* strategic thinking, 43–45; synthetic thinking and, 46
Apple Computer, 40
Aspirations, organizational: connecting others with, 154–155; examples of, 50; individual aspirations and, 56–60, 154–155, 221; leadership strategy and, 210; quantitative goals *versus*, 50; strategic leadership team aspirations and, 187, 221; in strategy making, 26–27; vision or visioning and, 50, 56–60
Assessing where we are phase: defined, 3, 20; for individual leadership development, 215–221; for

organizational change, 207–208; STRAT items mapped to, 236; strategic leadership teams in, 187, 189, 191; strategic thinking in, 56, 60, 62, 74; in strategy-as-learning-process framework, 20, 24–26, 31, 32, 33
Asset preservation, 116
Associated Press, 80
Athletic teams, 172–173
Attitudes, for leadership development, 222–224
Autonomy, balancing direction with, 96, 97–98, 165

B

Baird, L., 104
Banham, R., 16
Beatty, K., 15, 168, 173
Beer, M., 35, 40
Benchmarking Solutions, 16
Berlin, I., 35
Bias, confirmation, 80–81
Big-picture thinking, 76–77, 78
Blurring trend, 38–39
Board members, involving, 149
Bossidy, L., 82
Boundaries, 78; of strategic leadership teams, 180; unnatural relationships that cross, 139–141
Brand phase, Neoforma's, 23–24, 27, 29–30, 31, 33
Bristol-Myers Squibb, 50
Broad-based strategic leadership, 5–6, 37–39, 175. *See also* Strategic leadership

183–184; in strategic leadership
teams, 178; about strategy, 16
Communication systems, 194–195
Compaq, 11
Compensation system, strategic impact
of changing, 13. *See also* Reward
systems
Competencies, strategic leadership:
interconnections among, 41, 81–82,
83, 164–166; leadership development
for, 215–228; overview of, 3–5, 41; in
strategic leadership teams, 175–185.
See also Strategic acting; Strategic
influencing; Strategic thinking
Competition, internal, 129, 140–141
Competitive advantage. *See* Sustainable
competitive advantage
Competitive environment: agility and,
96; blurred boundaries and, 38–40;
drivers of new, 1–2; learning about,
225
Competitors, copying, 15
Complex and interdependent work:
drivers of, 1–2; strategic leaders' work
and, 18; strategic leadership teams
and, 183
Complex interactions, systems thinking
and, 77–79
Complexity: making common sense in,
67–68; strategic influence and, 123;
strategic thinking and, 45; systems
thinking and, 72–74, 77–79; trend
of, 2
Computer virus, 65–66
Confirmation bias, 80–81
Continuous-improvement team, 168
Continuous learning, 33–34. *See also*
Learning process framework
Control systems, 194
Conversations: about leadership strategy,
210; about organizational change,
213; with stakeholders, 152–154; in
strategic leadership teams, 178
Cooperative bidding, 146
Cost-cutting, unclear priorities in, 88, 90
Courage, 117–118
Courtney, H., 111
Credibility, 129, 133, 136–137;
measuring trust and, 138–139;
politics and, 143, 144; relationship
foundations and, 139

Cross-functional strategic leadership
teams, 174
Cross-unit collaboration, 139–141
Culture, 5; assessment of, 206–208;
changing, 207–209; in college case
study, 195–197, 200; cross-unit
collaboration and, 140, 141;
customer-focused, 29–30; in faith-
based health care organization case
study, 197–198, 201; fear in, 71–72;
impact of, on strategic leadership,
200–201; of knowing *versus* learning,
34; leadership strategy and, 28–29;
nature of, 192–193; power of
language in, 155; of risk-taking, 96,
99–101; signs of obstructive,
203–205; signs of supportive,
202–203; that supports strategy as a
learning process, 193–194, 201,
202–205. *See also* Climate
Customer focus, 29–30

D

D-Day invasion, 108, 110, 117–118
Data collection, for personal SWOT
analysis, 216–220
Deacon, S., 104
Debriefing: process, with strategic
leadership team, 224–225; Strategic
Team Review and Action Tool
(STRAT), 240–244
Decision making: nonrational aspects of,
86, 88; reframing in, 64–66; in
strategic leadership teams, 180–181;
uncertainty and, 108–116, 117–118,
119, 180–181. *See also* Priorities and
priority-setting; Strategic acting
Decisiveness, 83, 85, 96; acting with, in
face of uncertainty, 108–116,
117–118, 119, 180–181; of strategic
leadership teams, 180–181
Defense industry, 146
Deliberate and purposeful relationships,
137, 139, 165
Deliberate *versus* emergent strategy, 33,
91
Developing the Strategic Leader (DSL)
program, 6; business simulation of,
36–37, 159, 164, 184; on challenge of
gaining commitment, 123–124;
orienteering exercise of, 67–68,

About the Center
for Creative Leadership

The Center for Creative Leadership (CCL) is a nonprofit educational institution with international reach. For more than three decades its mission has been to advance the understanding, practice, and development of leadership for the benefit of society worldwide. CCL staff members conduct research, produce publications, and provide programs and assessment products to leaders and organizations in all sectors of society. Headquartered in Greensboro, North Carolina, CCL also has locations in Colorado Springs, Colorado; San Diego, California; Brussels, Belgium; and Singapore, as well as network associates around the world certified to offer selected CCL programs.

CCL annually serves leaders from more than 2,000 organizations—both public and private, including two-thirds of the Fortune 500. Each year, approximately 20,000 individuals participate in a CCL program and 100,000 professionals complete a CCL assessment. In 2003, *BusinessWeek*'s biennial special report on executive education ranked CCL 1st worldwide in leadership education for the third consecutive time. CCL also ranked 4th worldwide among open-enrollment programs and 7th among custom program providers in that report. In a 2004 *Financial Times* survey, CCL ranked among the world's Top 10 providers of executive education open-enrollment programs for the third consecutive time. CCL was the only institution ranked in that survey that focuses solely on leadership education.

Capabilities

CCL's activities encompass leadership education, knowledge generation and dissemination, and building a community centered on leadership. CCL is broadly recognized for excellence in executive education, leadership development, and innovation by sources such as *BusinessWeek*, the *Financial Times*, the *New York Times*, and the *Wall Street Journal*.

Open-Enrollment Programs

As today's business environment becomes more complex, CCL continues to help individuals, teams, and organizations address crucial leadership challenges through its portfolio of open-enrollment programs. Its one-of-a-kind individualized leadership program experience is built on a developmental model of assessment, challenge, and support. CCL combines 360-degree feedback, individual assessment, and personalized attention in a safe, confidential environment. In addition, many of its courses offer post-program development in the form of a three-month goal-setting process and follow-up, an assessment of behavioral change, or one-to-one interaction with a certified CCL feedback coach.

Visit http://www.ccl.org/programs for a complete listing of programs.

Customized Programs

CCL develops tailored educational solutions for several hundred client organizations around the world each year. Through this applied practice, CCL structures and delivers programs focused on specific leadership development needs within the context of defined organizational challenges, including innovation, the merging of cultures, and the development of a broader pool of leaders. The objective is to help organizations develop, within their own cultures, the leadership capacity they need to address challenges as they emerge.

Program details are available online at http://www.ccl.org/custom.

Assessment and Development Resources

CCL pioneered 360-degree feedback and believes that assessment provides a solid foundation for learning, growth, and transformation and that development truly happens when an individual recognizes the need to change. CCL offers a broad selection of assessment and development resources that can help individuals, teams, and organizations increase self-awareness, facilitate learning, enable development, and enhance effectiveness.

CCL's assessments are profiled at http://www.ccl.org/assessments.

Publications

The theoretical foundation for many of our programs, as well as the results of CCL's extensive and often groundbreaking research, can be found in the scores of publications issued by CCL Press and through CCL's alliance with Jossey-Bass, a Wiley imprint. Among these are landmark works, such as *Breaking the Glass Ceiling* and *The Lessons of Experience*, as well as quick-read guidebooks focused on core aspects of leadership. CCL publications provide insights and practical advice to help individuals become more effective leaders, develop leadership training within organizations, address issues of change and diversity, and build the systems and strategies that advance leadership collectively at the institutional level.

A complete listing of CCL publications is available at http://www.ccl.org/publications.

Leadership Community

To ensure that the Center's work remains focused, relevant, and has impact on the individuals and organizations it serves, CCL maintains a host of networks, councils, and learning and virtual communities that bring together alumni, donors, faculty, practicing leaders, and thought leaders from around the globe. CCL also forges relationships and alliances with individuals, organizations, and associations that share its values and mission. The energy, insights, and support from these relationships help shape and sustain CCL's educational and research practices and provide its clients with an added measure of motivation and inspiration as they continue their lifelong commitment to leadership and learning.

To learn more, visit http://www.ccl.org/community.

Research

For more than three decades, the Center has successfully transformed leadership knowledge into applications and practice into knowledge, thus becoming a forerunner in the advancement and understanding of leadership development. The extensive research work at the Center continues to be the impetus behind the development of new practical leadership tools for individuals and organizations. And likewise, what is learned in the classroom fuels new, timely, and cutting-edge research.

Find out more about current research initiatives on the Web at http://www.ccl.org/research.

For additional information about CCL, please visit its Web site at http://www.ccl.org or call Client Services at 336-545-2810.

More titles from the Center for Creative Leadership and Jossey-Bass.

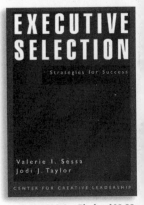
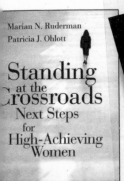

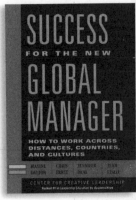